BENEATH THE SILVER LINING

Fans of the proper Dr. Frasier Crane couldn't believe it. Frasier accused of rape? But anybody familiar with the man behind the sitcom name knew that Kelsey Grammer has had more than his share of run-ins with the law and had twice served jail time. The first time was for failing to keep up child support payments for his daughter Spencer. Then, during the height of his *Cheers* popularity, Grammer was thrown in jail after being arrested twice within a few months, the first time for drunk driving, the second time for possession of cocaine. Considering his on-the-edge past, was it possible that Kelsey might be capable of doing something rash and impulsive and, as a result, lose everything he'd worked so hard to achieve?

But why?

What demons possess Grammer that seem to spur him to live on the dark edge so often?

KELSEY GRAMMER
•THE TRUE STORY•

Jeff Rovin
with
Kathleen Tracy
and David Perrell

HarperPaperbacks
A Division of HarperCollinsPublishers

HarperPaperbacks   *A Division of* HarperCollins*Publishers*
         10 East 53rd Street, New York, N.Y. 10022

First printing: November 1995

Printed in the United States of America

HarperPaperbacks and colophon are trademarks of
HarperCollins*Publishers*

❖ 10 9 8 7 6 5 4 3 2 1

KELSEY GRAMMER

INTRODUCTION

The story hit the papers with a vengeance—
from the tabloids to the *New York Times.*

Frasier star Kelsey Grammer is facing
investigations in New Jersey and
Arizona into allegations he had sex with
a fifteen-year-old girl last year.

"Mr. Grammer intends to be fully coop-
erative," said his spokeswoman, Shawn
Blake. "We have nothing to hide."

The girl, now seventeen, gave a statement Wednesday [November 23, 1994]
to Somerset County, New Jersey, prosecutor Nicholas Bissell, who said the case
will go forward.

"We will investigate that which she
has told us to see if we can get corrobo-
rative evidence. No decision has been
made about the charges."

The girl's father and stepmother, who live in Phoenix, went to police last year, but the girl did not support their allegations then. The encounter allegedly took place in June 1993 at a hotel gathering of friends Grammer attended. Authorities in Prescott, Arizona, are looking into similar allegations.

TV fans of the proper Dr. Frasier Crane couldn't believe it. Frasier accused of rape? But anybody familiar with the man behind the sitcom name knew that Kelsey Grammer has had more than his share of run-ins with the law, and has twice in his life served jail time. The first time was for failing to keep up child support payments for his daughter Spencer. Then, when he was at the height of his *Cheers* popularity, Grammer was thrown in jail after being arrested twice within the space of a few months, the first time for drunk driving, the second time for possession of cocaine. Considering his on-the-edge past, was it possible that Kelsey Grammer might be capable of doing something so rash and impulsive that as a result he'd lose everything he'd worked so hard to achieve?

But why?

What demons possess Grammer that seem to spur him to live on the dark edge so often?

It's no secret Kelsey seems to have a highly developed self-destruct mechanism. In the past, just when success was blossoming and life was turning rosy, something had happened to sidetrack him: he had gotten arrested, or he'd married someone he would later describe as mentally deranged. He often let his addictions take over his life. The paths Kelsey has walked have been strewn with heartbreaking minefields, casualties, and upheavals starting from his earliest years, as though he's been conditioned nearly from birth to endure the rockiest road imaginable.

But rarely has anyone had a past so full of pain and tragedy.

ONE

Allen Kelsey Grammer was born February 21, 1955, on the lazy tropical island of St. Thomas, in the Virgin Islands. His eccentric father, Allen Sr., was an American expatriate who owned and ran a local bar and grill while his mom, Sally, stayed at home. The elder Grammer felt alive in the tropical paradise and involved himself in local politics, sharing his views via a magazine he published. In the light of the multicolored sunsets, Allen Grammer also gave music lessons to local children.

While her husband flourished, Sally was wilting—she never took to island life and was increasingly homesick for the States. In 1957, when Kelsey was only two and his sister, Karen, just eight months old, Sally filed for divorce.

On March 22, 1957, Sally Cranmer Grammer testified in the divorce proceedings, and the life she described was one of isolation and longing.

Kelsey's mom told the court she and Allen had

been married in Maple Shade, New Jersey, on Valentine's Day, 1954, and had moved to St. Thomas a short time later.

"My husband has always been self-indulgent, very opinionated and would never accept any of my opinions or my ideas, or my desires, but always wanted his wishes to be done on all occasions.

"He was uncompromising in his attitude and his opinions.

"He would say, 'Let's do something,' and I'd say OK. But then five minutes—or a week—later, he would say, 'No, I decided not to do that.' It happened with practically everything he did."

Sally testified that Allen often complained he wasn't happy with her and that arguments were common.

"He practically argued about everything. He would argue with me on the way I was raising the children; on the way that I was doing the shopping for both places; the way I dressed; the way I talked; the way I walked."

When Sally would finish her day's work at around nine o'clock in the evening, Allen would drop her off at home, then head back out.

"He didn't wish to remain at home," Sally said. "He would go back downtown and then after he had closed his bar he would go out on the town, staying [out till] three, four, five o'clock in the morning."

His night-owl hours bothered Sally, and she asked him why he had to go out, but she never got an answer. She was also unhappy with him as a father.

"He didn't seem to have any attitude at all about

[the children]. When the first baby was small, when he would come home in the afternoon, he would say, 'Well, give Kelsey a bottle and put him in the bed.' . . . So oftentimes I would, and now Kelsey is older and you can no longer shove him in the crib all the time, but he still takes the same attitude."

Sally also admitted Allen had once slapped her, but what seemed to bother her most is how he acted around the house. At the time of the divorce, Grammer had apparently lost the bar and was a stay-at-home.

"Lately, since he's been home, he's either worked on a so-called house-plan that he has changed every day for six months approximately, or he's indulged himself in playing music or something or [he'll] simply lie down on the bed and go to sleep."

The divorce records also recount an incident that took place in March 1956 at Allen's bar and which impelled Sally to leave St. Thomas and return to her parents' in New Jersey for a while. After dropping Sally off at home, Grammer went back to work only to find the bar a shambles.

"The next day he got a very threatening note," Sally recalled. "He was also warned by several people that they heard that I was being threatened, and the children were also going to be threatened, and the next day he said, 'I think you better go home.' I left four days later."

Years later, Kelsey would explain that the family suspected that his father had run afoul of some "political" enemies, and perhaps this account by his mother lends credence to that.

Sally stayed in New Jersey until August of 1956.

While there, she gave birth to Kelsey's sister, Karen, on July 15. During their separation, Sally and Allen wrote each other long letters and realized they wanted to give their marriage a second chance.

"We decided that if I came back in the fall we might be able to work it out and have it on a better keel," Sally said. "When I came back I was able to entertain and have a very little bit of social life, more or less make a home, and it was very, very pleasant for a month and a half or two months.

"Then he began to develop back into this same thing, going out late three or four nights a week, being silent, unindulgent in conversation, exchange may be [sic] four words a day.

"When I asked what was wrong he said, 'I don't know.'"

Sally couldn't figure out what she had done to deserve this silent treatment. She begged her husband to tell her what she should be doing, but he answered with silence.

During her testimony, Sally admitted that the stress caused by her relationship with Allen sometimes caused her to take it out on Kelsey and Karen.

In December 1956 Grammer left St. Thomas on a trip to the United States with his friend George Hogue. They were to sail a boat back to the Virgin Islands.

"I was against it a little bit," Sally admitted. "And he knew that, but my reasons were entirely personal, so I put them aside and I said, 'All right, go.' I said, 'I know you want to go, and I know that you will never forgive me if I don't let you go.' And I also knew Mr. Hogue wanted him with him. They were good friends.

"I had one letter from my husband while he was in the States, before they left. In that letter, he said that the main reason he left was that he felt he had to get away; that he couldn't stand it any longer; that he had to get away from me and the children; that he wanted to think about us, and he felt he just couldn't do it with me because he couldn't converse with me on it, or anything.

"They left New York on the fourth [of January] and no one heard from them at all for three weeks, just about. And at that time we found out that the boat had been sunk, that two survivors, my husband and another boy, were picked up and on their way to Germany."

But the shock of hearing her husband was headed for Europe was not the worst. Allen wrote her from Germany, saying that despite his terrible experience of sinking at sea, "he still felt fairly good being away from me."

When Grammar finally returned home, Sally says he picked up where he left off, treating her with quiet disdain. One day they got into an argument over the children, with Allen accusing Sally of not being able to handle them.

It was the last straw. Sally had been humiliated enough. She testified that she didn't believe there was any chance of reconciliation. If they got back together, in a few months' time it would happen all over again.

Sally moved out on March 19, 1957, and filed for divorce—called a separation agreement in the Virgin Islands—the next day.

The court agreed with Sally that there was no reasonable prospect she and Allen could reconcile their differences. Her settlement included $100 a month child support until Karen was five, then $150 a month until she was 15, and $200 monthly until she was eighteen.

They split jointly owned property, ironed out insurance benefits, and tied up the loose ends caused by a marriage being dissolved.

On the twenty-ninth of March, 1957, Judge Herman E. Moore finalized their divorce. Sally was free to leave. She took her children back to New Jersey. Struggling to support her young brood, Sally moved in with her parents.

Kelsey's years in New Jersey turned out to be the happiest of his childhood. He and his maternal grandfather, Gordon, became inseparable.

"He was the only male figure I had," Kelsey says thoughtfully. "He pretty much replaced my father simply by physically being there. He was a voice of wisdom on how to get through a certain day that didn't feel so good."

Gordon was an oil company executive who readily took on the role of mentor.

"Dinner was always a time for conversation," Kelsey recalls. "After the dishes were cleared, my grandfather and I would talk over what happened that day at school and what was going on in the world. He would also tell me stories about fighting at Guadalcanal during World War II. He was the most interesting man—a retired army colonel who was a liberal conservative and a situational philosopher."

Gordon helped his grandson navigate the waters

of childhood, from teaching him the basics of how to be a gentleman to helping him deal with bullies at school.

"I remember when I was eleven and in fifth grade complaining to my grandfather that some kids were picking on me and really bothering me," Grammer recalls. "He said, 'Kels, you see a bug, you step on it or walk around it.'

"I was like, 'Oh, yeah, thanks for all the help.' At the time, I didn't understand what he meant, but now, of course, I do—if something is bugging you, let it go. In most cases you don't need to create a confrontation, just walk away from it."

Grammer put that wisdom to use when fending off barbs thrown at him because of his unusual name.

"When I was growing up they called me Elsie the Cow," Kelsey says. "And because of my last name, Graham Cracker. Elsie the Cow Graham Cracker. At first, I sort of minded. Then I thought to myself, 'Why am I worried about them?' Fortunately I had the sense that maybe I just shouldn't bother with people who couldn't get past my name. That turned out to be a very astute observation on my part."

An artifact from his childhood casts an interesting light on the inner longings of an eight-year-old Kelsey. It's a map he drew of a place he called Grammerland, a kind of mental theme park.

"There were some really cool rides," Grammer says with a smile. "Water rides, a big Ferris wheel, and a roller coaster. It was very green and very neat-looking."

But the main attraction, according to Grammer, was the Hall of Windows.

"It was a place where you could put your eyes in front of a device that reveals who you really are—and teaches you how to love yourself again. That would have to be the park's main attraction."

In 1967, when Kelsey was still eleven, Gordon decided it was time for his family to permanently fly south for the winter. He bought a house in Pompano Beach, Florida, loaded up his wife, daughter, and grandkids, and set off for the Sunshine State.

The thought of moving back to the surf and sand thrilled Kelsey. The early years he spent in the warm breezes of the Virgin Islands may have been brief, but they had made an indelible impression on him, and part of Kelsey must have felt as if he were going home. But the youngster's happiness was cut jarringly short.

Just one week after moving into their new home, Gordon died. The sudden, unexpected death sent Kelsey reeling. His anchor had been snatched away from him, and now he was drifting alone, trying not to sink under the weight of suddenly being looked at as the man of the house.

"After my grandfather died, I took over," Kelsey says. "I took care of things—from that point on I always would. After his death, all I dealt with was my mother and my sister and my grandmother—three different generations of women who pretty much relied on me to play son, father, husband, and child all at the same time. That was a little confusing for an adolescent growing up."

Aware that her children's most important, not to mention only, male role model was gone, Sally arranged for Kelsey and Karen to go visit their father—and his new family—in the Virgin Islands. Apparently the thought that Allen was a virtual stranger to them never crossed her mind.

The summer after their grandfather's death, Kelsey and Karen were reacquainted with their father and met his new family. Not long after his divorce was final from Sally, Allen had met a former New Yorker named Elizabeth—also known as Skeets to her friends. Skeets had worked at *Look* magazine before moving to the Virgin Islands, and by the summer of 1967 she and Allen had four children. It was the first—and only—occasion Kelsey would spend time with his half-siblings, Betty, John, Billy, and Stephen.

Interestingly, there's disagreement as to how long Kelsey and Karen visited their dad. In interviews, Kelsey's recollection is that he spent a couple of months on St. Thomas, but other family members peg it closer to a couple of weeks. However long the visit, Kelsey saw that his father still pursued his jack-of-all-trades lifestyle.

"By the time Kelsey and Karen came down to visit that summer, Allen had sold the bar and grill he had owned while married to Sally," says a family friend, who also notes that nobody can quite remember the name of the restaurant.

Having left behind the food business, Allen veered toward more creative outlets. During that summer of 1967, the senior Grammer ran a music shop, published a magazine with the help of Skeets, and became a local personality as a deejay at the local station, WSTA.

"The music shop came about because of Allen's love of music," says the family friend. "He was a very good musician and played the trombone and string bass, both with and without a bow. At the radio station, he did a sort of variety entertainment show. He played music, hosted a call-in section, did skits, and would read excerpts from authors like Ambrose Bierce."

The magazine dealt with local St. Thomas issues, and some feel Allen's involvement in the island's political scene may have made him some dangerous enemies.

"Allen would write various commentaries, some of them political in nature," the friend recalls. "Allen actually even ran for the Senate once, mainly to encourage people to split votes—to vote for the individual rather than just the symbol of a party."

In a picture taken by Skeets that summer, Kelsey is standing next to his bearded, stocky father, with his sister and half-siblings all gathered around. The picture was taken on the grounds of Allen and Skeet's lagoon-front home, with the enticing waters of the Caribbean sparkling in the background. In retrospect, it's a poignant family portrait. Of the seven Grammers smiling into the camera, only three survive. But, still untouched by the tragedies yet to come, Kelsey's smile is the widest, and he seems genuinely happy to be there.

Less than a year after that summer vacation, death would visit a member of Kelsey's family a second time.

Shortly before midnight on April 25, 1968, Allen Grammer thought he heard something, or someone, outside. Leaving Skeets behind, he ambled outside to take a look. Skeets recalls hearing the sound of a gunshot and hearing Allen calling out for help.

"He said, 'Call the police! I've been shot!'"

Before she could grab the phone, another shot rang out, killing Allen almost instantly. He was only thirty-eight years old.

Later, police would arrest a local cab driver.

"He was found not guilty, by reason of insanity," Elizabeth, who is now sixty, says today. "I think he might still be incarcerated in a hospital in St. Thomas, but I'm not sure. I think for a while he was allowed out so he could go do some work."

Following the senseless murder, Skeets packed up her four young children and took off for Spain, staying there a year before she could bear returning home to face life without Allen.

Kelsey's reaction, at least on the surface, was far less emotional.

"I really didn't know him that well," he says. "Other than the couple of months with him the summer my grandfather died, I hadn't seen him since my parents divorced—I wasn't really aware of who my father was. When we found out he'd been killed, I remember feeling a bit detached. He was a nice guy, but it was a very short experience—and then he was dead."

Grammer seems to have made an effort to adopt his grandfather's intellectual curiosity and verbal skills, but like many kids, especially those from broken homes, Kelsey didn't realize just how much he was a chip off the old block. It's obvious he inherited his father's love of music and penchant for performing. What Allen Grammer did for a few thousand radio listeners in St. Thomas, Kelsey would eventually do on TV for millions of viewers.

But it would be a while before Kelsey would realize performing was in his blood. Still grieving the loss of his grandfather and unsettled by the mix of feelings caused by his father's murder, Kelsey found comfort in the sea and took refuge in surfing's physical exertion and the intense concentration it required. When he was on a wave, no other thoughts could intrude. Plus it was an activity he could pursue on his own.

"I guess it had to do with my grandfather dying," Kelsey admits. "I became a recluse, a loner, and was alone a good deal of the time. I liked to surf and then go home and meditate. But surfing was a big, huge part of my life—early on it was the *biggest* part of my life and spiritual development, more than almost anything else. It had a lot to do with my sense of well-being. And God. That intimacy with the ocean is still a big thing for me. I took up sailing later, and even now there's no greater feeling than when you leave the sight of land and you're in the presence of what's central to the universe."

But back in Florida as a teenager, surfing simply offered him a comfort zone in which he didn't have to deal with anything or anyone else. Besides his lingering sense of loss, Kelsey was also confronted with the painful adolescent trauma of not fitting in.

"I went through the usual sort of peer ostracism," Kelsey says. "But after a while, finally, I really didn't care about them very much."

Grammer attended the rather posh private Fort Lauderdale coed prep school, Pine Crest. As he got

older Kelsey got his first taste of the release offered
by alcohol. It allowed him to relax a bit and lower
the barriers for a moment. Despite the feelings of
alienation that remained in his head, outwardly
Kelsey was still able to have a good time.

"We had wild, all-night parties and drank too
much," recalls one of Kelsey's classmates from their
prep school days.

Others remember a different Kelsey.

"He was a rebel who was smart and sweet—but
he was also an outsider."

But it was at Pine Crest where all the different
Kelseys discovered acting. To his amazement,
standing onstage before an audience gave him the
same rush of adrenaline and blanket of ecstasy that
surfing did. And it all began as a fluke.

When he was sixteen, an English teacher convinced him to take a role in the school production
of *The Little Foxes*. Up till then, if Kelsey had any
thoughts of following a career in the arts, he would
have been leaning toward music. Blessed with a
good singing voice, Grammer had broken out of his
shell enough to perform in several concerts spon-
sored by local Methodist and Catholic churches.

He also considered a much more conservative
path. In what was little more than an attempt to
remain spiritually close to his grandfather, Kelsey
also toyed with the idea of applying to Annapolis,
where he could follow in his grandfather's military
footsteps. But both music and the military were
quickly put on the back burner the first night
Kelsey performed in front of an audience.

"I was taking my bow after the first performance
and I thought, 'Now this I can do for the rest of my

life, and it would still be really like surfing,'" Kelsey remembers. "Performing onstage was exciting and engaging, and it had a kind of freedom. It's adolescent in a way.

"Surfing was my faith. It's like a functional realization of Zen philosophy. But acting is also moment-to-moment, if it's any good. You just go with the wave of a play and you ride it and you don't necessarily conquer it. You spend time together."

Plus acting gave Kelsey a wonderful excuse to escape. Later he would use the same rationale to lose himself in drugs and alcohol.

"I do try to run away from things sometimes," Grammer admits. "Hence I became an actor—acting gives you a great opportunity to express yourself honestly without being accountable for it. See, it's not really *Kelsey*, it's *that character*. You get off the hook."

By the time he graduated from high school, Kelsey was desperately looking to escape. The pressure of being man of the house had begun to weigh heavily on the teenager, and he reacted by rebelling against the women in his life. That he would leave Florida was inevitable; the only question was where would he go.

"It was a controlling environment," he says of his home life. "When I left, I was amazed at the myth that had been concocted about how indispensable I was. I was raised a Christian Scientist. The credo 'Sin, disease, and death are not real. Will is infinite mind and its infinite manifestations' is an idea that got me through a lot. I was a classic case of how you subvert childhood pain. I had an image of

myself as being immortal, of trying to outdo everyone I knew—like Errol Flynn."

As it turns out, when Kelsey left the Sunshine
State, he was leaving for good, never to live there
again. The lingering reminder of his grandfather
would forever taint the state for him, his love of
surfing notwithstanding. There was always Hawaii.
Kelsey was ready to move on to the next chapter of
his life.

Interestingly, while Florida never lured Grammer
back, he was drawn to return to St. Thomas years
later.

"Kelsey has only been back to his father's house
twice since Allen died," says a family friend. "The
most recent time was two years ago, when Kelsey
was thirty-eight. His father was murdered when he
was only thirty-eight, and Kelsey felt the urge to
come back when he was the same age his father
had been when he died. Somehow it gave him a
sense of completion."

"Yes, I went there the summer of 1993, and I can
see why I might want to live there someday,"
Kelsey muses. "It may have something to do with
another life—who knows? It's peaceful, soothing,
calming, clean—I like the tropical climes and feel at
home in them."

But in the summer of 1973, with his hair
bleached blond by the sun and falling to the middle
of his back, Kelsey was an unsettled young man in
search of a home.

TWO

Like a bird going home to roost, Kelsey packed his suitcase full of jeans and T-shirts and headed back north to New York. Life in the big city was an eye-opener for Grammer, who found himself in awe at the possibilities offered, the intensity of people on the street, and the sheer mass of humanity squeezed into Manhattan's twenty-two square miles. For Kelsey, the fast pace New Yorkers are accustomed to seemed even more breakneck compared with the low-key—downright meandering in contrast—Florida lifestyle he'd grown up with.

Grammer hit the streets of the Big Apple as thousands of other hopeful actors before him had—but unlike most others, his attitude was not one of quiet desperation. Even then, Kelsey maintained and projected what could be seen as protective, self-anchoring confidence—or as arrogance. He was not someone anxious to please or willing to do anything for the sake of either promoting his art or even just putting food on the table.

"I decided it was better to say 'fuck you' without having any fuck-you money in the bank," Kelsey explains. "You know, being able to tell people where they can go when you *really* need the job is more important than saying no when it doesn't matter.

"I've turned down lots of jobs, including a good-paying porno job I was offered when I was eighteen."

Grammer, who in those youthful days boasted a long golden mane of hair that cascaded past his shoulders, was offered ten thousand dollars to work on a porno film called *The Bermuda Triangle.*

"The deal was to film on a yacht that would sail through the Bahamas for three weeks, during which I would 'do' two lovely women," Kelsey reminisces. "For me, it just seemed wrong, even though I desperately needed the money—I had no food. But I just couldn't."

Part of Grammer's rationale, interestingly enough, has a very feminist sound to it.

"It's true I looked pretty good then," Kelsey admits. "But I always thought the thing that people should find interesting in you is your *brain.* That's what *I've* always found interesting in people. I've been with different people in my life who, by regular standards, might not be considered all that attractive. But that wasn't what I was into anyway. It's the intellect and what you see behind the eyes that make people attractive to me."

And that is what he's always hoped, even as a good-looking eighteen-year-old, that other people find interesting in him.

"The most fun is if the whole package is there," Kelsey goes on. "But you do need the whole package. I've had opportunities to be with people who were physically stunning but so mentally *unengaging* that it was impossible to find them attractive, except on a visually objective—but emotionally removed—level."

Translating the Kelsey-speak, that means "cute but dumb." And even Grammer must appreciate the irony of his comments, considering that a few of his more-celebrated relationships later on in life are hardly remembered for their intellectual dimensions. It's the old struggle of idealism against reality. Kelsey would grow into a man torn between two worlds. But at that moment his future seemed wide open.

Having passed on his chance to be the John Holmes of his generation, Kelsey considered his options. While many would-be thespians might start out by looking for a reputable acting class in which they could begin to work on their craft, Kelsey decided to go for it in a major way and start at the top. Despite having no references and only two years of high-school drama productions under his belt, Kelsey made his way to Lincoln Center, the home of the prestigious Juilliard School.

In front of the imperial and imposing producer-director John Houseman, Grammer chose a Willy Loman scene from *Death of a Salesman* for his audition. To Kelsey's pleasure, Houseman welcomed him in, apparently believing Kelsey had *"earned it."*

One of Kelsey's classmates, playwright Tom Waites, says that even then Grammer showed definite signs of eccentricity.

"It would be twenty degrees below zero outside and Kelsey would be wearing sandals—shorts and sandals," Waites recalls. "But Kelsey was also the type of guy who would look out for other people. If you were having a tough time, he'd sense it and come over and ask what was up."

"In retrospect, I learned a lot," Grammer says now. "It takes about five years to digest everything. They teach you from scratch—how to walk, how to talk, just everything. But it's worth it."

But in 1975 Kelsey's appreciation for Juilliard's curriculum wasn't as finely tuned. Or maybe he simply concocted a reason to push himself out of the school's safe nest. Security was not something Kelsey was used to, and we all tend to distrust what we don't know. Whatever his subconscious motivation, two years after Houseman welcomed him with open arms, Kelsey was tersely asked to leave.

"They threw me out, really," Kelsey explains. "At Juilliard, there's a cut every term. I made it through two full years before they told me it wasn't working out. Which I already knew—it was a perfectly good reason. It's just that I had lost interest in some of the things that were going on there. They kept asking me if I really wanted to be an actor. I knew I did, but I didn't want to go on trying to prove it to them using their recognized formula.

"So it was fine. We weren't getting along, but there was no uproar or trauma, and the parting was amicable."

Kelsey also admits that he felt it was time to move on, an apparent acknowledgment of the restlessness that seems to be his constant companion.

But before leaving, he was called in for one last chat with the formidable Houseman.

"I didn't really know John Houseman even though he was running the drama department," Kelsey says, which maybe indicates one of the fundamental problems he had at Juilliard. "But he would have a kind of closure meeting with those of us who got kicked out. So Houseman called me in for this last meeting and said a great thing to me. He told me to read the great novels.

"It's a way of giving yourself information about a world that doesn't exist anymore—of relationships, mores, and styles of association that don't exist anymore. As an actor, if you don't have that kind of information, you'll never be able to portray people in that world with any kind of authority and style. His advice was dead on. And I had the insight to follow his advice."

Change and transition were nothing new to Grammer, so he didn't consider the end of his association with Juilliard to be a negative event or a handicap to overcome. Nor did it seem to undermine his confidence—he saw it simply as the beginning of a new chapter. But not everybody shared his water-off-a-duck's-back style.

"It wasn't a big deal to me—but it was to everyone else. My girlfriend at the time just freaked out. She came from a family where her father was an insurance salesman," he says, as if that held the key to explaining why she was so upset.

"Our relationship had been at a very serious stage, but after I left Juilliard it was as if her whole world collapsed. Maybe she thought it said something about my ability to earn a living, or my responsibility. It surprised me that leaving school caused that kind of reaction in her."

Needless to say, that relationship would soon be history. But in a short time, Juilliard, a breakup with a girlfriend, or any other part of daily life would suddenly become completely unimportant to Kelsey.

"The year I got thrown out of school was the same year my sister died," Kelsey intones quietly. "She was the sixth of seven victims in a Colorado murder spree. That was a real big one.

"That's when I lost my faith."

The all-too-real nightmare—and unquestionably the biggest loss—that haunts Kelsey's life began on the evening of June 30, 1975. Karen Grammer, then eighteen and living in Colorado Springs, was sitting outside the restaurant where she worked as a waitress. According to reports at the time, three men (who, it was later revealed, had been planning a robbery) pulled up to the curb where she sat, opened the door, and dragged a screaming, struggling Karen inside.

The car sped off, tires squealing. In reconstructing the crime, detectives determined that Karen was taken to a nearby apartment, where at least one of the men raped her. Afterward they hustled her back into the car, drove to a dark alley near the Arvada House Apartments, and pushed her out of the car, dumping her on the ground. Then one of the men ordered Karen to raise her head. When she did as she was told, thinking her ordeal was almost over, the man reached down, cut her throat and stabbed her, then drove off, leaving her to die.

Somehow, summoning superhuman strength,

Karen crawled to a nearby trailer park before bleeding to death. Her body wasn't found until the next morning.

At the same time his sister was taking her final breaths, Kelsey was back in Pompano Beach, visiting his family and looking forward to seeing his sister.

"The last time I talked to her was when I was in Florida," Kelsey recalls. "It was the summer. She was living in Colorado Springs but said she was going to come down and visit after the Fourth of July. That meant I would see her on her birthday, which was July fifteenth.

"When the Fourth of July passed and we didn't hear from her, everyone started to get a little worried. On the sixth of July we finally contacted the police in Colorado Springs. A day later they called back and told us there was a Jane Doe in the morgue and they believed this Jane Doe was Karen. They said she had been killed the first of July."

Stunned and in a state of disbelieving shock, Grammer took the next plane out to Colorado Springs. As the man of the family, the burden of confirming his sister's death and bringing her body back to Florida fell onto his shoulders.

"At this point, I still didn't know what exactly had happened to my sister," Kelsey continues. "When I landed, I was picked up at the airport by a policeman, who turned out to be very nice. Driving into the city, we started talking about death. I told him I had experienced death before in my family but nothing that compared to this."

No doubt in an attempt to offer sympathy, the

officer told Kelsey he himself had recently experienced a terrible loss when his best friend died in a helicopter accident. Even in the worst of circumstances, shared misery promotes a kind of camaraderie. Knowing the policeman had experienced a similar loss offered Kelsey a macabre sense of comfort—at least until the time Kelsey had to go in and identify the body, and learned the details of her senseless, brutal murder.

"I was pretty numb—and a little violent—after that. I blamed myself for not being there to protect her," Kelsey says, alluding to the pressure he felt to be the man of the family. "I had always taken care of her. Maybe I felt that in some ways I was supposed to be a father to her."

That September, police issued warrants for the arrest of three suspects in Karen's murder—and would also investigate the trio for a string of at least four other murders.

"Before Karen's death, I had an almost blind, naive faith in God and the universe. I could see goodness and joy almost everywhere I looked. But Karen's death changed that. It was not a good time—but interestingly, I wasn't abusing anything."

"He still cries about her," says an old girlfriend, Cerlette Lamme. "I don't know if he blames himself, but sometimes I think he wishes he could have been there to save her."

"There is nobody biologically closer to you than a sibling," Kelsey says, trying to explain the closeness he felt to Karen. During all the years of family upheaval, through the loss of his grandfather, Kelsey always assumed Karen would be there for him—and he'd be there for Karen.

It's hard not to wonder how much of Kelsey's despair was exacerbated by feelings of guilt. More death and violent homicide had touched his young life than that of most people twice his age. His grandfather's death robbed him of his father figure and a strong, supportive male role model. His real father, whom he visited for two weeks the summer after losing his grandfather, seemed a stranger to him. When news of his father's murder reached Kelsey, he admittedly felt detached. Even at twelve, he probably knew he should feel *something*, but to this day all he can say is that his father seemed like a nice man. He was never able to muster any emotion resembling the strong feelings he had for his grandfather, despite his father's tragic end.

Kelsey's emotional hands were not clean concerning his sister, either. When talking about the "oppressiveness" of his home life as a teenager, he included his sister along with his mother and grandmother. He admits that he felt expected to be everything to all of them, and he talks about the weightiness of the pressure he felt from that expectation. He also felt during his teen years that his mother and grandmother had let him know he wasn't living up to their expectations. And Kelsey resented being told he was a disappointment, knowing that in their eyes—including Karen's—he wasn't doing the best he could be doing.

It's impossible to grow up without at some point wishing a sibling would just go away and leave you alone. But after her unfathomable violation and murder, any sense of resentment, any barbed thought he had ever harbored as a youth toward Karen, must have come back to haunt him as petty, wasted, and unretrievable. Remorse, on top of the straightforward grief a surviving family member struggles with, becomes an additional crown of thorns. Sometimes it lasts a lifetime.

"That was the worst part of my life," Kelsey says with level understatement. "It opened a huge hole in terms of my emotional stability. In terms of my life, I'll never completely get over it. There are nights I wake up and feel the pain creeping back in.

"It will simply never be over."

After the funeral Kelsey couldn't stay in Florida. He needed to get away from the family home, which was too full of memories, and from his mother and grandmother's grief—his own was simply too overpowering. So he returned to New York, but no change of scenery could ease his agony. Nearly blind with grief, Kelsey sleepwalked through the following months.

"I lost a lot when Karen died, and the year after her murder was the worst I've ever lived through. I was *way* down there. I was depressed to the point of despair, to where I could barely stand up. I'd find myself standing at the refrigerator door and two hours would have passed. It took about a year to where I could even think there might be a reason to go on."

Considering that the mere act of getting out of bed required a major effort, it's not surprising that his career was equally paralyzed. Grammer figures he must have gone on at least a hundred auditions but didn't get so much as a local commercial. To put food on the table and to keep a roof over his head, Kelsey drifted from one struggling-actor-type job to another: he waited on tables, worked construction, unloaded fishing boats in Rhode Island, and painted offices. As it turns out, it was his ability as a handyman that proved to be a turning point in his life and career.

"One day I was painting the office of a casting agent named Ellis Rabb. He looked up at me from his desk and then asked, wasn't I an actor? I told him I was."

Getting to know Kelsey, Rabb got an idea and made Grammer an offer he couldn't dream of refusing. Through contacts, Rabb set him up with a job at San Diego's famed Old Globe Theater. Kelsey was a young man going west—if he could only find a way to get there.

The only transportation Kelsey had was a rickety old motorcycle. So he borrowed $140 from his grandmother, tuned the cycle up and got it in running condition, then hit the road to California. It was a hair-raising cross-country journey, and it was a toss-up whether the motorcycle would make it or die in the middle of Death Valley. For once Lady Luck smiled on Kelsey, and he puttered into San Diego in one piece.

It was just the therapy Kelsey needed to get past his emotional catatonia. At the Old Globe, Kelsey could immerse himself in classical as well as modern theater and allow himself time to heal. During this time Kelsey also honed his considerable dramatic skills, and learned to use his voice, which had matured into a deep, resonant tool.

"It was like completing college," Kelsey says, looking back. "I had a ball. Because of that time, the stage will always be my first love. It's what I think establishes you as an actor."

The workload was a welcome relief to Kelsey, and it was during his three seasons at the Old Globe that his confidence was cemented and he prepared himself to face the world again. It is where he honed his "gifts," as he likes to call them. But after two years in the coastal beauty of San Diego, Kelsey's restlessness erupted again, looking suspiciously like a fear of being too comfortable. So Kelsey, now a twenty-five-year-old man, packed up, took a deep breath, and made his way back East.

Unbelievably, the Grim Reaper wasn't finished with Kelsey's kin. Although he had spent only a brief two weeks with them the summer after his grandfather died, Grammer was still stunned by the news that two of his half-brothers—Stephen and Billy—died in a freak diving accident on June 1, 1980, almost five years after Karen's death.

"It was pretty gruesome," says an acquaintance. "The two of them were scuba diving in the waters around St. Thomas when Billy failed to come back to the surface. After waiting around a little while, Stephen became worried and dove in to look for his brother. Stephen suffered an embolism while in the water and basically choked on his own vomit. Stephen's body was recovered but Billy's body was never found. The authorities who investigated the accident are pretty convinced he was eaten by sharks, which are plentiful in the area waters."

"I had a kind of distant reaction to their deaths," Kelsey admits. "Of course I remembered them from the time I'd spent with them, but I felt very removed from it."

Plus the last thing Kelsey needed was anything

that would reopen the barely healed wound of his sister's death. He was finally moving forward again at full steam, and so he shucked off the news of his half-brothers' deaths out of self-preservation. He had his sights set on acting and needed to stay focused or else risk sliding back into his personal abyss. He made Broadway his next mountain to conquer.

"I had to defeat New York," Kelsey says. "I had felt a bit overwhelmed by it before."

The Great White Way was better the second time around. Grammer more than survived doing occasional television roles but mostly theater, including out-of-town stints in Minneapolis and Buffalo regional theater companies and the American Shakespeare Theater in Stratford, Connecticut. But most important to Kelsey was his triumph in New York, which included stage roles in *A Month in the Country*, *Macbeth*, and *Othello* (the last with James Earl Jones and Christopher Plummer).

It was a heady period, and Kelsey felt for the first time as if his life was turning around. Now he could enjoy good fortune instead of misfortune. He felt comfortable enough to consider settling down and creating a family sanctuary for himself. Kelsey was in this frame of mind when he met a pretty young dancer named Doreen Alderman while attending a party for a show in which he was appearing.

"When I met Doreen, I'd been on the road with a touring company and I was getting tired of seeing a lot of different women," Kelsey recalls. "I fell in love with Doreen, but at the same time, I really wanted to start a family."

They were married three months later, on May 30,

1982. But marital bliss slipped through Kelsey's hands before he could even figure out what went wrong.

"It was like we had one great day—our wedding day. After that, it got rocky. It seemed that I didn't know her quite as well as I thought I did."

But part of Kelsey's reason for marrying was satisfied. In 1983, Kelsey and Doreen became the very proud parents of Spencer Karen—her middle name in memory of Kelsey's sister. But even the joy of having a child together wasn't enough to save the marriage, which eventually disintegrated into a rancorous breakup. Unable to go through the emotional wringer anymore, Kelsey and Doreen finally separated in 1984. To this day, though, Kelsey still speaks in bitter tones about the time between the breakup and the divorce, six years later.

Legal wrangling became a way of life. One court order instructed Grammer to pay $52,000 in child support.

"I was asked to give her more money than I had ever made in a year," Kelsey says with heat.

Eventually, his unwillingness or inability to comply with that order prompted a judge to sentence Grammer to a ten-day jail term, which was later suspended. Little did he realize it was only the beginning of legal troubles that would dog him for years to come.

Averse to letting his personal life interfere with his blossoming career, Kelsey stayed concentrated. Although his focus was on the theater, he still did occasional television appearances, and ironically it was the small screen that gave Kelsey his first taste of wide recognition.

In 1984 Grammer was cast on the daytime drama *Another World* in the small role of Dr. Canard.

"It wasn't a major, major role," says *TV Guide* columnist Michael Logan. "In fact, you don't even find his credit in some of the soap reference books."

But Kelsey was still doing well enough to land himself an audition for one of the most sought-after prime-time television roles being offered in 1984. A new character, originally conceived as a boyfriend for Shelley Long, was being introduced on *Cheers*—Dr. Frasier Crane. The sitcom had already been on the air three years and had established itself as one of the classiest comedies on the air, which is why even though the character was scheduled to appear in only six or seven episodes, the role was much sought after.

Typically, when Kelsey heard about the upcoming audition, his attitude was a take-it-or-leave-it one. Theater had seduced his soul, and that was where he was content to stay. But work was also work, and six or seven episodes on a hit series would pay more than what he earned in a year on the boards.

"Everyone was very secretive about it," Kelsey recalls. "No one could see the script—it was like being involved in industrial espionage. To be truthful, I had never even seen *Cheers*, so I had no idea what exactly I was auditioning for."

Finally an envelope containing his pages of dialogue was delivered to Kelsey, and to his surprise, once he got a look at the character he connected immediately. "I knew him. I *understood* him."

Grammer blew the competition away. Suddenly, and with very little emotional preparation, he was headed west again.

It's ironic that someone who claimed to have such ambivalence about pursuing a television career still managed to shine so brightly when reading for the role. Actors often say the biggest hurdle to overcome in the audition process is controlling any feelings of desperation. Worrying too much that you won't get the job or won't do a good reading—whether the worry is born of financial need or fear that failure to be hired for a certain role is a reflection on either one's talent or one's worth as a human being—often becomes a self-fulfilling prophecy.

Grammer explains the philosophy he developed that enabled him to overcome that most basic obstacle to success.

"A long time ago I coined a term—requisite disrespect—which has to do with both the way I work and the way I live. You can't take too much too seriously. Not the acting, but the *process* of getting the chance to act. You can go to an audition feeling intimidated or you can go in and show them that you are what they are looking for. It's disrespect for yourself, basically—for your own sense that you're more important than the work."

Rather than feeling as if he had just won the lottery, Kelsey had mixed emotions about the new road he was about to take.

"I was very, very nervous about doing television, the idea of committing to it," Kelsey admits. "You can't help but think to yourself that you're going to get trapped–'Oh, my God, what if I never get to play any other character but Frasier Crane again?'"

Grammer comforted himself with the belief that the job was a short-term detour from the theater.

Besides the fact he was hired to appear in only six or seven episodes, once in L.A. he also got the strong impression that Shelley Long wasn't overly fond of the Frasier character.

Not expecting his time on *Cheers* to be of any long-lasting consequence, nor wanting it to be, Kelsey wasn't afraid to speak up about—and speak up in defense of—Frasier, the man he felt he knew so well.

He wasted no time protesting the relationship between the psychiatrist and Long's character, Diane. Originally it was written that Frasier was dating Diane at the same time he was acting as her therapist.

"The one thing that was clear about Frasier Crane, regardless of whatever shambles his own life may be in, is that he's a *great* psychiatrist," Kelsey explains. "Dating Diane would be unprofessional—and he simply wouldn't do that."

Thanks to his input, the producers went back to the drawing board and came up with an introduction that turned out to be much funnier—Frasier initially meets Diane when he has to prevent her from coldcocking another patient with a croquet mallet.

His years in the theater, and the confidence and trust in his "gifts" that time had instilled in him, would serve Kelsey well in Hollywood, giving him enough moxie to fly in the face of a top-ten show's brain trust and tell them they were wrong.

Despite his apprehension over entering the Hollywood community and his reluctance to put his theater work behind, there were things Grammer wasn't sad to leave behind in New York,

even for the short term—most notably the ever-
escalating animosity with Doreen.

But rather than being an unfortunate mistake
not to be repeated, his painful and emotionally
draining relationship with Doreen was just a preview of what was to come.

THREE

The success and financial freedom *Cheers* afforded Kelsey also let him pursue some of his more hedonistic impulses—namely, drinking and drugs. Kelsey would later admit he had started using cocaine in 1979 during his time in San Diego. The city was close to the Mexican border, and drugs flowed freely into San Diego, moving north to the other California counties. Grammer found cocaine particularly appealing because he felt it turned his brain *on*, rather than dulling it the way downers such as marijuana tended to do.

He also developed a strong taste for gin and tonic, and took the concept of happy hour very seriously. His tape-day routine seldom varied: He would show up dressed in his usual jeans, tennis shoes, and T-shirt, and go through the final rehearsal and an afternoon cocktail before letting the makeup and wardrobe people transform him into the dapper Frasier.

In addition to finding the good life amid the warm, dry southern California ocean breezes, Kelsey also found love again.

Grammer had barely unpacked his bags before he was already checking out the local theater scene. He picked up where he had left off in New York by immediately landing a role in a production of Shakespeare's *Measure for Measure*. Now Kelsey was really having his cake and eating it, too. During the day he was making big money on *Cheers* while still being able to work on plays at night thanks to the nine-to-five nature of TV sitcom work.

Measure for Measure was being staged at the Mark Taper Forum, one of three theaters that make up L.A.'s Music Center complex. The Taper is the smallest of the theaters, an intimate space where the audience is very close to the actors onstage. During one performance, Kelsey did a double take when he spotted a pretty blond lady in the audience. He was so smitten that he wrote her a note during intermission asking her out and had the stage manager deliver it.

The lady who stole Kelsey's heart and sent his libido racing was Cerlette Lamme, a former skater with the Ice Capades.

"I still have that note," Lamme admits. "At the time he was separated from his first wife and living in some hole in the wall in Venice. He used to drive around on his motorcycle wearing shorts and a crazy shirt.

"That's the guy I fell in love with."

But not everyone was equally as enchanted with Grammer—particularly *Cheers'* leading lady, Shelley

Long. And initially there was some unspoken resentment from other series regulars as well.

"When they created Frasier, they did so with the specific intention of having a character they could write intelligent humor for," says a writer. "With Shelley and Ted, they had to come up with cutesy dialogue, while Norm and Cliff represented the more lowbrow humor. One of the reasons [Kelsey] got the job is because his obvious intelligence came through at the reading. They were impressed with his intellect.

"But this did not go over so well with the cast at first—especially when Kelsey was able to just nail the dialogue. It got under Shelley's skin more than anyone's. When Kelsey says he 'got the impression' she wasn't fond of the character, that's like saying the plague is a slight infection.

"She did everything in her considerable power to undermine Kelsey—all in the name of what was best for the show, of course. During the weekly read-through, Kelsey would often get some of the biggest laughs. Except from Shelley," who sat there with a Stepford-wife smile glued to her face.

"After the read-through, Shelley would march out the door after the writers very pointedly. The next day when Kelsey came in, he'd discover many of his lines had been cut because Shelley had thrown her weight around. And inevitably the producers had to appease her. Her trump card was the lingering threat that she would just leave the show. At that time they thought Shelley was one of the main foundations, and worried the show might not survive if she left. So they kowtowed to her pettiness."

Driving Grammer off the show seemed to become Shelley's personal crusade, and she never missed an opportunity to let him not-so-subtly know it.

"She made his life miserable for a while," the writer says. "At one rehearsal, during the time the Frasier and Diane characters were dating, Shelley announced that she had been thinking. 'You know . . . I'm thinking that Diane would not really want to continue a relationship with this guy. I think we need to create another character for Diane to become involved with—and write a final episode for Frasier.'

"Kelsey just sat there, totally stunned. So did everyone else. Later on, he admitted just how upset he was—something along the lines of, 'You know, this is my only job right now, and this bitch is trying to get rid of me.'

"By sheer force of will, and talent, Kelsey stood his ground. He made it work. He got laughs out of dialogue that would have made others in the cast throw their hands up in surrender. It became a battle of wills, and Kelsey simply wasn't going to let Shelley push him out the door without putting up a fight.

"And what's funny is that the whole battle with Shelley made Kelsey one of the inner circle because it bonded everyone in their mutual dislike of Shelley."

So in the end, Kelsey won when it was Shelley who eventually left. *Cheers* was a hit, and Kelsey was a hit on *Cheers*. What had started out being a limited run had turned into a career move, forcing Grammer to relocate permanently to the West

Coast. Kelsey might have called New York home, but he wasted little time acclimating to his new climate and surroundings. In many ways, Kelsey and Los Angeles were made for each other—casual, laid back, and open to suggestion.

When it became clear that Lamme was more than just a short-term fling, Kelsey rented a run-down four-bedroom house in Van Nuys, an area in Los Angeles's sprawling San Fernando Valley. His choice of home was curious considering that Grammer was making more than enough money to afford, if not an upscale abode, then at least a well-kept home. One friend contradicts that thinking, claiming Kelsey was in a financial tar pit.

"For many years on *Cheers*, Kelsey wasn't making big, big money—not the kind of money people thought he was. He was definitely having money problems, and it wasn't that his lifestyle was extravagant. He didn't drive fancy cars or live in a postcard-pretty house. But he had expenses that were eating him up. He would always complain, 'It sucks to work every week and spend all my money.' Back around 1985 to 1987, a lot of money went to his ex-wife. But a lot of it went up his nose, too. His life was already in disarray."

Or perhaps his surroundings were simply a reflection of Grammer's internal life.

"My friends called it Fort Grammer," Kelsey says of the eyesore that was his house and property.

And its uninviting grounds certainly did create a barrier few would want to cross. A cyclone fence defined the perimeter of the property, which boasted an ample but neglected yard overgrown with weeds killing any grass that dared get in their way. A pile of bricks leaned against the house front, which resembled the cartoon character Sluggo's house, with its tattered bamboo shutters hanging crookedly and its windows propped open. Some of the neighbors complained about the sounds of constant partying.

Kelsey's taste in cars seemed to match his taste in houses and landscaping. Decorating the driveway was a stable of cars that would make Rent-a-Wreck proud—an Oldsmobile, a dented Cadillac, a truck, and an old Triumph, which would figure in another Kelsey setback a few years down the road.

The street address was scrawled by hand on a piece of cardboard tied to the front gates, which were usually closed to keep out the world. Inside wasn't much better. The furnishings included an old couch and a beat-up coffee table. Visitors to the house remembered the stale smell of cigarettes and animals that hung in the air.

"The house had a gate and there was a sign out front that said 'Grammer Ranch'—it was plain disgusting," says a regular visitor to the house. "I don't know how anyone could live like that, especially with the money he made. The yard looked like there had been no work done on it for two or three years—everything was dead because nothing had been watered. All that was left was dirt and weeds.

"And of course not only did you have to walk through piles and piles of dog doo outside, but inside too. They had something like a dozen dogs. The house was really disgusting. The furniture was so badly beaten up it looked like he had gotten it out of some trash Dumpster.

"There were tables with books underneath to

hold them up because the legs were broken. The sofa had a huge sag in the middle and stuffing was sticking out of holes everywhere, plus the wood tables had cigarette burn marks all over them. Empty gin bottles were lying everywhere, even under tables. And in the kitchen, dirty dishes were everywhere.

"It was impossible to believe a TV star making a huge amount of money, regardless of what else he spent it on, would live like this. The first time I was there he said, 'Don't mind the house—the maid didn't show up.'

"I looked around and asked, 'For the past four years?'

"He laughed, but the bottom line is, it was a total pigpen."

The one area that was noticeably not neglected, in fact seemed a centerpiece, was the well-kept, fully stocked bar. Kelsey made it no secret he enjoyed offering his friends a cocktail in the afternoon. Not to mention morning, noon, and night, too.

One friend of Grammer admits Kelsey would often start drinking very early in the morning.

"He'd take a drink of gin and say, very dramatically, 'Good morning! That's my gasoline to get going!'"

Grammer was also developing a dangerous reliance on cocaine. It had become an insidious presence in his life. He saw it as his payoff, a reward to himself for success.

"Without question, Kelsey was a wild man," his friend says. "The Kelsey I hung out with back during the early days of *Cheers* was just an absolute, raging wild man. I mean, this guy was living life *too* fully. There were definitely times he needed to stop partying because it started to affect him in terms of showing up for work. Plus, he went through a lot of depression."

The friend admits that he too did a lot of drugs.

"Yeah, I confess that I went through my bouts with cocaine. I hate to say it, but Kelsey always had a pocket full of cocaine. I'd go to his dressing room after a taping and we'd do coke in his dressing room. But never before taping. And he only did this with his closest friends."

Although Grammer's friends insist Kelsey never used cocaine before performing on *Cheers*, that technicality cut little ice with network honchos. There were instances when his well-known excessive partying threatened his future on the show, even though the producers on *Cheers* were loath to let him go.

"I remember times when his behavior definitely jeopardized his job," the friend says. "There were times he didn't show up for work. The producers told him that if he didn't come in the next day, not to bother coming back at all. They told him he'd better get his act straightened up."

Cerlette admits she knew Kelsey was doing drugs—because they had done them together.

"But I didn't like it, so he eventually did it without me."

And for a while, Grammer simply did without Lamme. The two briefly split when Kelsey pursued an affair with model Teri McJessey. But the stunning beauty claims to have nipped the romance in the bud because she couldn't abide Kelsey's heavy-duty partying. So it was back to Cerlette, who stood by her man and ignored his drug abuse.

His drinking was another matter for concern. He often showed up with a mind-splitting hangover.

"He dragged into work some mornings looking like hell and in a foul mood," said one crew member. "His face would be bloated, and he'd have bags under his eyes. He'd come right out and tell people to leave him alone because he had tied one on the night before."

"He was out of control," says another friend. "There were times when he was beyond the point of knowing where he was and what he was doing.

"One time I was out with him and we were on our way home. I'm driving down the freeway and he was so wasted he started to open the door and step out! I screamed and slammed on the brakes. He could have killed himself—it scared me half to death. Kelsey had this silly look on his face and asked, 'Oh . . . we're not home?' I said, 'No, we're not home, you fool.'"

Even years later, Grammer would still be in a state of denial about how the drug was affecting his life. In 1993 he told a reporter from the *Washington Post* that he had enjoyed his "little addiction."

"I had a lot of fun with it. It just got a little out of hand and was not improving my life," he said, making it sound like some Oscar Wilde comedy of manners.

To nearly everyone who witnessed other drug-related incidents, Grammer's addiction was a tragedy long in the making.

"Before he and Cerlette moved to Fort Grammer, Kelsey lived with a buddy in Venice," says the friend. "It was a real pit, too. I remember once they shut off his electricity, and his phone was disconnected because he didn't pay the bills. This was a TV star. And he almost got convicted for not paying the rent."

But Grammer had plenty of money now to buy drugs.

"He was sharing his cocaine with everyone, which got to be pretty costly pretty quick. And the thing is, it was obvious he wasn't happy. He walked with his head down. I'd also say at the time he was an alcoholic.

"It seemed like every time he took a step forward in his life, he would immediately take two steps back. And it stayed that way as the years went by on *Cheers*. He continued to stay out late partying on alcohol and cocaine and it continued to cause him problems. Why, I don't know, other than it was some form of escape. That's what drugs are, a pain suppressor."

Some of Grammer's friends are convinced Kelsey's self-destruction was rooted in his sister's death more than anything else.

"Over the years Kelsey has talked several times in interviews about his sister's murder, but what he's never talked about publicly is *why* Kelsey always says he feels guilty, why he feels that he should have been there to protect her," says a *Cheers* buddy. "What he has confessed to close friends is that on several occasions, Karen had called Kelsey up and asked him to come out to Colorado Springs. He kept promising he would, but kept putting it off. He was too busy getting on with his own life. Then before he knew it, his sister's life was over.

"He's never forgiven himself for that—and probably never will."

Whatever the reason for his recklessness, it was only a matter of time before his personal excesses collided with the rising star of his career.

That time began in July 1987, when Grammer was stopped and cited for driving without a license and for being under the influence of alcohol and drugs. The event didn't create much of a ripple, as DUIs in California are not an uncommon violation, especially among high-flying celebrities.

On July 13, Grammer pleaded no contest to the drunk-driving charge. As part of the sentence, he was ordered to complete an alcohol-education program and was put on probation. He was ordered to appear in court at a later date to provide proof to the court that he had indeed completed the sentence.

Other than some teasing from friends and coworkers, the citation seemed an embarrassing but insignificant life event. Kelsey seemed suitably humbled and had appeared sincere in court when he agreed to attend the alcohol-education program. The incident troubled Lamme, who convinced Kelsey to start attending Alcoholics Anonymous meetings. Feeling contrite, he did—for a while. But as the weeks passed, his promises to the court, and to Cerlette, faded into a distant memory.

Until April 14, 1988.

That night two uniformed policemen, Officers Akana and Crawford, were cruising the streets in Studio City, a tony area west of Van Nuys that holds the distinction of having more actors as residents than any other community in the country.

Driving along in their conspicuous black-and-white unit, the officers spotted Grammer's red Triumph traveling on Riverside Drive and noticed the car's license plates were expired.

They pulled Grammer over, intending to write him a ticket, which the court might have later dismissed if he registered the car within a certain number of days. But this would prove to be no routine stop. When asked to hand over his driver's license, Grammer gave the policemen a learner's permit.

Back in the black-and-white, they ran a computer check on Grammer and discovered he was driving without a valid license. The computer also revealed that Grammer had an outstanding traffic warrant for speeding. This was not good news for Kelsey. LAPD officers seldom let you go if they find an outstanding traffic warrant. In fact, they're known for gleefully hauling drivers off to jail if the computer shows they have let a jaywalking ticket go to warrant.

When Akana and Crawford walked back to Grammer's car, they asked him to get out of the car to study him more closely. On second look they noticed that his eyes appeared bloodshot and his face was flushed, and the officers thought his coordination appeared impaired. They also smelled alcohol on him. They told Kelsey he was under arrest for the outstanding warrant.

Before putting Kelsey in the back of the black-and-white, the officers checked the rear seat and floorboard and, according to their report, found it "clear of contraband."

The officers took Kelsey to the North Hollywood

police station, and in accordance with the routine they followed with all prisoners, they checked the back of the patrol car after Kelsey got out to make sure nothing had been left behind. It wasn't uncommon for prisoners to try to stash anything they didn't want a body search to turn up during the booking process. The backseat was clear.

Inside the station, Grammer was twice given a breathalyzer test, and both times it indicated that Kelsey's blood alcohol content was .03 percent—well below the legal limit. From the North Hollywood station, Grammer was taken to the Van Nuys station "for further investigation." Feeling like a ball bouncing around in a legal pinball machine, Kelsey must have started getting panicky the longer he was in police custody. The arrest report tells what happened next.

"Upon defendant exiting the police car at Van Nuys Station, Officer Akana discovered a folded paper bindle containing a white powdery substance resembling cocaine."

In classic addict fashion, Kelsey was immediately remorseful. In fact, he was so moved he felt compelled to write the officer a note.

"That cocaine was in my pocket. I felt stupid. I should have just told you I had it. You deserve better than that. I would like to apologize to you."

The powder subsequently tested positive for cocaine. The bindle contained only a quarter of a gram—barely enough to make a few "lines" to snort—but it was more than enough to put everything Grammer had worked for in jeopardy.

Kelsey had finally fallen into big-time trouble—even though he didn't realize it at first.

This second arrest sent off alarms and caused others, including his bosses at *Cheers,* to start looking a little more closely at Kelsey. But Grammer was nothing if not an excellent actor. He also exuded a boyish, mischievous charm—a good boy who'd done a bad thing. Because he was genuinely liked and likable, it was hard for people to be harsh with Kelsey. Nobody insisted he stop and explain why he seemed to be doing everything in his power to destroy himself. Not even Cerlette could make herself look far enough beneath the surface to see the truth.

Grammer appeared in court, and in order to avoid going to jail, he asked to enroll in a ninety-day substance-abuse program under an option the state of California offers first-time drug offenders. But Grammer never bothered to go to the program. He was too busy having a good time.

Kelsey sightings at local L.A. hot spots and watering holes were still commonplace in the weeks and months after the second arrest.

"I saw him at a Beverly Hills restaurant one afternoon when he drank half a bottle of Gordon's gin, . mixed with tonic," says one patron. "He was drunk, but not out of control."

One of his party buddies laughs when thinking how Kelsey had told the police he "occasionally" snorted cocaine.

"I saw him snort as well as drink a *lot.* In fact, it was surprising if I ever saw him sober. One time I found him passed out at the Sports Arena, which is an arena in downtown Los Angeles where the Clippers basketball team plays."

On this particular night, another eyewitness

reveals, Billy Joel had given a concert. "The event was over and I was leaving when I saw this guy face down in the grass. Unconscious. At first I didn't know who it was, just some guy. But when I got closer he started looking familiar. I walked over and sure enough, it was Kelsey. He looked up at me and said, 'Please take me home. Please get me home. I'll do anything.'

"He was so drunk he could barely communicate. Then he threw up on the grass. I let him roll over, then went to find his limo driver to make sure he got home."

Others leaving the arena looked on in shock as the man they knew as Frasier Crane tried to gather himself up.

"There were other people around and he told them he had had too much to drink and couldn't find his limo," says the concert-goer. "Then he staggered off into the parking lot."

But for the most part, except for a handful of shocked eyewitnesses, viewers at home had no idea Kelsey Grammer's life was like a plane plummeting to earth. But they soon would.

After Grammer's cocaine arrest in April, his attorney, Bobby Diamond, had succeeded in having him placed into a court-ordered substance-abuse program. It was the easiest way to clear his record and minimize the scandal. But Diamond made one mistake—he left it up to Kelsey to register for and attend the program.

"Had I known Kelsey was like that, I would have sent a bodyguard with him," the attorney says now. "I had no idea he would let it slide. You tell him he has to do something and he loses track. You know he's an incredibly intelligent person, so when he tells you he signed up for the program, you believe him. Most people do.

"A friend of mine in the district attorney's office called me and said, 'Bobby, the guy hasn't even done the diversion program.'

"Then I found out he hadn't done anything he was supposed to do."

FOUR

On February 6, 1990, Grammer was scheduled to appear in court and provide proof he had satisfactorily finished the alcohol-education program he had been ordered to undergo after his arrest in July 1987. He was a no-show, and a bench warrant was issued. Somehow it went unnoticed by the courthouse press.

He was also scheduled to appear on May 2 in Van Nuys Municipal Court for a court-ordered "progress check" as part of his cocaine possession case. He was a no-show there too. So on May 2 an arrest warrant was issued by Van Nuys Municipal Court Judge Aviva K. Bobb—ironically, the same judge who had ordered Kelsey to enter a substance-abuse program after his arrest for cocaine possession.

Grammer's high-wire act was finally about to crash to the ground.

Deputy District Attorney Andrew Diamond (no

relation to Grammer's lawyer, Bobby Diamond) confirmed that Kelsey was, in essence, a wanted criminal.

"He failed to comply. He didn't show up in court, and now there is a bench warrant out for his arrest. Anybody can get busy, but you can't be so busy that you can't sign up for a program after seven months.

"He's not going to be allowed to weasel out of this. Our policies apply to everyone—to Joe Lunchbucket as well to him. We're not going to ignore the situation just because he appears on a television show. And should he get himself arrested again, he'll miss cocktail hour at *Cheers* for a while."

Grammer's attorney, Bobby Diamond,claimed his client was out of the country and unreachable. And he was at a loss to explain why Kelsey had failed to comply with any of the court's orders.

Others could speculate why.

"He hadn't fallen off the wagon—because he was never on it," says someone familiar with Kelsey. "He was on the lam, carousing like a wild man. While he was supposed to be attending rehab classes, he was out drinking and partying.

"One night at the China Club, he was stoned out of his mind, dancing with a blonde and then dancing alone. He was unshaven and looked like a mess."

On May 10, eight days after the second warrant was issued, Grammer finally surrendered to the court. His excuse was almost laughable. Basically, it was that he forgot. Kelsey claimed his most recent court date had slipped his mind because had been preoccupied with the ill health of Cerlette, whom he now called his fiancée.

KELSEY GRAMMER • 55

Judge Bobb was unimpressed, telling him, "We all have other responsibilities."

Good thing he also forgot to mention that the reason his attorney couldn't contact him the week before was that Kelsey and Cerlette had been vacationing on a cruise to Mexico.

He was released on $7,500 bail and ordered to return six days later to face the music for failing to attend his alcohol-education class. Looking wan and shell-shocked, Kelsey's disheveled appearance caused whispering among courthouse personnel, who said it showed disrespect for the court. To others, he looked like a man whose partying had finally caught up with him.

On May 16 Grammer was back in Van Nuys Municipal Court facing the same judge he had spurned before, Judge Patricia Schwartz. This time around, he was neater and a little more together, but it was way too late to change the court's impression of him. Although one person tried. In a testament to the affection felt for Grammer by his *Cheers* peers, costar Kirstie Alley appeared in court to speak on his behalf, and she asked the judge that Kelsey be spared jail so he could seek help from Narconon.

"I am here because I work with Kelsey and I think there is hope and he needs help," Alley, a self-described former cocaine addict with a $400-a-week habit, told the judge. At that time Alley also happened to be the international spokeswoman for Narconon.

"Eleven years ago I was a drug addict and I was very irresponsible—I did similar things to what Kelsey did. This is the program that worked for me and I've been drug-free for eleven years, not a few weeks or six months like you're used to hearing people say. I am very concerned Kelsey take full responsibility for what he did, which was drive while drinking."

What made Alley's plea all the more poignant was that her own mom had been killed by a drunk driver in 1981. But she had strong feelings, and concerns, for Kelsey's future, and sincerely wanted to help.

Judge Schwartz was unmoved and declined to order Grammer into Narconon in lieu of jail, saying it was an option he could pursue on his own. She then threw the book at him. For failing to comply with the terms of probation for his 1987 drunk driving offense, she sentenced him to thirty days in jail and ten days community service working with Caltrans, the agency that controls expressway maintenance in Cailfornia. He was also ordered to attend the ninety-day alcohol-education program he'd agreed to way back in 1988 as part of his probation.

Kelsey was ordered to finish his Caltrans work—which consisted of tasks such as pulling weeds around an off-ramp of the Ventura Freeway—by July 25 and to complete the alcohol education program by August 23. And this was only his punishment for the drunk driving offense—sentencing for his cocaine possession arrest was still to come.

"It's probably the world's record sentencing for a first-time drunk driving conviction," Bobby Diamond wryly noted.

Although his castmates showed unwavering public support, they had known for some time that Kelsey was like a train headed over a cliff.

"He'd been showing up on the set obviously not sober and acting just plain nutty. Plus he'd run off to his dressing room or the bathroom every few minutes. It had gotten well past the point of discreet. And his mood swings were becoming just impossible to deal with," the writer said.

So the decision was made to force him to put the brakes on. After conferring with each other, several of the cast, including Ted Danson, George Wendt, Rhea Perlman, Kirstie, along with a couple of the producers, planned a surprise attack. They were going to do what's called an "intervention." Basically, friends and/or family sit a person down without warning and one by one tell him what his behavior has been and that each person there believes he is an addict or alcoholic in need of treatment.

They carpooled together to Kelsey's house at six A.M. on a Saturday morning, all poised to go through with a decidedly unpleasant activity. As a group, they knocked on Kelsey's door and waited. And waited.

He wasn't home.

"Apparently he was still out partying," the writer says. "After having pumped themselves up to do it, not finding him home really deflated everyone. Later, a couple people tried again on another day. This time they found Kelsey home, doing cocaine. Before they could say much of anything, he asked them to leave his house."

The intervention had been a colossal failure. Instead of his castmates forcing him to take responsibility, it was the court that finally did. But again, it says something that his *Cheers* coworkers still rallied behind him when all was said and done—even though they'd been not only unable to help, but angrily turned away.

"Kelsey is a great person," Alley said later. "He goes all over the country all the time doing benefits and helping people out. It's sad that the one person Kelsey has not helped is Kelsey."

"Everybody liked Kelsey," agreed a friend. "There was nobody on that set who didn't like him—except when Shelley Long was there. But she hated everyone and everyone hated her.

"But Kelsey is a great guy. When we went out and he was approached or bothered in public, I never saw him rude. He was always a nice man who takes time for people. Clearly, underneath everything he has a really big heart and is a nice guy.

"When Kelsey would go out with a group of friends, he's the one who makes sure everything is nice. He's the one who makes the evening better. For example, one night we were going out to go to a football game and before leaving he had the limo driver run to the store and pick up six bottles of champagne and put them on ice.

"The point is, he's very unselfish, very sharing. Kelsey's a great guy who would never screw anyone over. I think he got a bad rap. He just went through some tough times and a lot of depressing things. He had a drug problem. Well, who in Hollywood doesn't?"

Actually, the truth is that most people in Hollywood don't have a drug problem. What's most interesting is that via the very words his friends use to defend him, their own destructive enabling comes screaming through. Not to mention a dangerous level of rationalization that only helped Kelsey dig a deeper hole for himself to be buried in.

"For some reason the press picked him to sensationalize a drug problem," the friend says, falling back on the old blame-the-messenger syndrome. "But he was no worse than a lot of other actors I've known."

Grammer was given a week to get his affairs in order before turning himself in on May 24. Like other inmates, Grammer was eligible to have his sentence reduced for good behavior—and because of an emergency release program for nonviolent offenders that had been instituted to reduce jail overcrowding.

Los Angeles County sheriff's deputy Richard Dinsmoor said: "Grammer is not going to be treated any differently than any other inmate. But he probably won't be housed with the general population out of concern for his safety because of his celebrity status."

It was hardly a great consolation for Grammer.

Carrying a toothbrush in his shirt pocket, Grammer surrendered to the court May 24 to begin his jail term. Trying desperately to regain control, Grammer told the court he had enrolled in the alcohol-education program and had already done one day's work with Caltrans on May 23. Decked out in a hard hat and an orange Caltrans vest to prevent harried drivers from running him over, Kelsey had spent a day doing what for him must have been hard labor, cleaning the area around one of the off-ramps of the Ventura Freeway.

Once remanded into custody, Grammer was

taken by sheriffs from the Van Nuys courthouse to the L.A. County Jail, where he was booked and fingerprinted, then given a standard jail-issue orange jumpsuit before being escorted to his living quarters. His cell was ten feet by twelve feet, with a wall-mounted toilet and a mattress on the floor. Even for someone as proudly bohemian as Grammer, the severity of his surroundings must have come as a shock, with the turn his life had taken finally hitting home. At least for the moment.

"Anything that he could use to hang himself has been taken away from him," said a deputy, explaining standard procedures. "He's given a razor blade to shave only in the presence of a jailer, who stays with him while he shaves, then takes the blade back when he's done."

Those around Grammer had begun damage control soon after his first court appearance. The effort went into high gear during his jail time, partly because by this time there was disturbing speculation that his job on *Cheers*—which was paying him $40,000 an episode—may have been hanging by a thread.

Attorney Bobby Diamond offered an explanation for Grammer's failure to appear at any of his prior court dates that most people would dismiss as Hollywood make-believe. Remember, he had been arrested for drunk driving in 1987, and it was now 1990.

"Kelsey was counting on his girlfriend—she normally would have reminded him," Diamond said in his client's defense. "He leads a life where people continually tell him what to do the next day. To say, 'See you in February 1990'—he just can't keep that kind of calendar.

"He's a very bright, creative actor who blanks out when it comes to keeping appointments. He didn't realize how serious his situation was."

Not at first, but by the time he was commuting back and forth to court, it started to hit home, especially in terms of the effect it might have on the series, both because of the publicity and morale-wise. Kelsey was appropriately apologetic to the people he worked with on *Cheers*, cast and crew alike. He was man enough to stand up and say he was sorry.

"I have to go to court. I'm really sorry and I hope it doesn't have any grave consequences for the show."

Diamond's it-was-really-the-girlfriend's-responsibility spin came about because during the early days of their relationship Lamme had helped manage Kelsey's business dealings. Although she didn't anymore, apparently Diamond felt it was still Cerlette's job to remind Kelsey of his multitude of court dates and other important appointments, such as enrolling in court-ordered programs.

Interestingly enough, Grammer's lawyer is himself very familiar with the excesses of Hollywood. Bobby Diamond, fifty-one, is a former child actor who is best known for playing Joey in the 1950s series *Fury*. After the series went off the air, he continued acting for years—all the way through law school, in fact—appearing as a guest on various television series including *My Three Sons*, *Wagon Train*, and *The Fugitive*. He laughingly admits he uses his dramatic background in the courtroom.

"A really good trial lawyer must captivate his audience," Diamond explains. "In court, your audience is the jury. If you can get the jury laughing, it's almost impossible for them to find your client guilty."

Unfortunately for Kelsey, judges aren't that easily amused or swayed.

Showing just what a sense of humor he has, Diamond—with law degree and bar certification in hand—became a regular on *Divorce Court*, as attorney Steve North.

"I took it seriously for the first year, but then I started having problems when they asked me to finish my closing argument in fifteen seconds. It suddenly occurred to me that this wasn't real."

That must have been a relief for Kelsey.

"In fact, some of the *Divorce Court* cases got downright weird," Diamond goes on. "One case involved circus performers who were cheating on each other. The husband was making it with the lion tamer while the wife was making it with the monkey trainer. After that I wore a tie with Superman on it—and they never even noticed until after the taping was over. That was my last year on *Divorce Court*. I guess they didn't like my new attitude."

There were those who would also have advocated a serious attitude adjustment on Grammer's part during those dark days in 1990. Then again, there were others, such as Cerlette, who continued to run interference for him. Despite Kelsey's increasing disdain for the tabloid press, Lamme gave a tearful interview to a tabloid paper shortly after Kelsey surrendered to begin his jail term.

Cerlette, then thirty, tried to absorb some of the heat—and make Kelsey's actions seem somehow less irresponsible than they were—by saying he had been too overwrought with concern about her health to remember something like a court date.

"I have seizure syndrome," Cerlette explained, which was caused by a sinus condition, but which had eluded diagnosis from October 1989 to March 1990. "He's been real worried about me. I know it's no excuse but it's true. There's still bloodstains on our rug that we can't get out from when I would have seizures. I'd be standing up, walking around the house, and the next thing I know, I'm in the hospital.

"I got the worst ones when Kelsey was not around. A girlfriend would find me and call the ambulance. All this year I've been sick and Kelsey's been taking care of me. I had a brain operation April 20. When I got my stitches out, Kelsey was so happy I was well, he took me on a two-week cruise down the Mexican coast. That's why he wasn't in those rehab classes."

Despite her fierce loyalty to Grammer, Cerlette never accompanied him to court, not even on the day he was to begin his jail sentence.

"There weren't any family or friends around to see him off to jail because that's the way he wanted it," Lamme explained. "There was no sense in going to court just to see him taken away. It would have made me real upset. It was hard enough just saying good-bye. He was resigned to it, but I wasn't—I started to cry uncontrollably.

"I may never see Kelsey again," she added, which made little sense considering that she had just announced they'd been celebrating the return of her good health with a cruise to Mexico.

On a more levelheaded note, Lamme talked about Kelsey's stalwart attempts to make good on his sentence.

"He did that one day of community service—pulling weeds—and he was already tired of it after one day. He's got nine more to go and he's not exactly looking forward to them."

His sentence also posed another potential problem for Grammer—this one with his soon-to-be-ex-wife, Doreen. The last thing Kelsey wanted was for his record, especially the drug charge, to somehow affect the custody arrangement he had for Spencer with Doreen. A mid-August hearing was scheduled with his estranged wife—the divorce was still not final—so Kelsey made contact with Doreen, just to make sure she wasn't furious with him.

Quite the contrary, in fact. Doreen was worried about Kelsey and told friends that the last time she had spoken to him "he was very depressed. He claimed not to have any idea how to cope with everything."

Kelsey coped rather well, it turns out, because while in jail he learned that things could be worse. A lot worse. While incarcerated, Grammer met Christian Brando, Marlon's son, who had been arrested in connection with the shooting death of his sister's boyfriend. Because of his name, Christian was also being housed in the isolated "celebrity wing" of the jail. After hearing what Christian faced, suddenly his jail time seemed lightweight. Later, he expressed his sympathy for

Christian, who eventually went to state prison after plea-bargaining to a lesser charge than murder.

If there was a silver lining, it was that Kelsey's job was secure. Not only were Kelsey's *Cheers* buddies standing by him, but the producers were also willing to give him another chance. James Burrows, the show's executive producer and director, announced Kelsey's contract had been renewed, saying, "I'm looking forward to another great season with a very talented actor."

The news must have been a relief to Grammer—as was the support shown by castmates Woody Harrelson and Kirstie Alley, who traveled to downtown Los Angeles to visit Kelsey in his bleak jail surroundings. Lamme also was relieved his job wouldn't suffer because of his legal entanglements.

"Kelsey re-signed his contract, so he'll definitely be back on the show next year. They've all been the most supportive of anyone, but then, he goes to work every day on time and prepared," said Cerlette, revealing her own highly tuned sense of denial. "*He's* not the one they ever have problems with. If you talk to the people who know Kelsey, they'd all tell you the same thing—he's a good guy and he works hard. He makes mistakes, that's all."

Once again, a Greek chorus singing Kelsey's praises piped up.

"You can't believe how great he is—everyone in the industry will tell you he's phenomenal," claimed a friend. "His acting skills are top-rate. If you had compared him to everyone else on *Cheers,* he was overqualified for the job. His background in movement, diction, [and] voice and his résumé engulfed those of Woody Harrelson and Ted Danson.

"He's a total actor. He's always into characters, especially Shakespearean. There's not a greater Shakespearean actor I've ever known—personally."

Apparently John Gielgud, Richard Burton, and Laurence Olivier were not cronies.

"Kelsey's famous for standing up in a bar and reciting Shakespeare. Many times after *Cheers* finished taping, which was on a Tuesday night, we would go down to a bar just down the street from Paramount Studios, where we filmed. We'd hook up with the guys from *Wings*, who also shot that night. We'd sit around drinking and getting tipsy until late. Then Kelsey would entertain us all. Everyone had seen his recitation of Shakespeare, so all the other actors would encourage him to do it. Sometimes he would even stand on a table."

That Grammer loves the classics cannot be disputed. In fact, during his summer hiatus from *Cheers*, he would participate in various California Shakespeare festivals. It was his love for Cerlette that became increasingly questionable.

Cerlette either was blindly loyal or suffered from selective vision when it came to the continuous hints that Kelsey was cheating on her. When she caught him red-handed, she dismissed it as "a mistake."

One time Cerlette was forced to confront the issue of another woman when photos taken before his jail term showed him cozying up to a pretty young woman.

"Kelsey was photographed with some blond girl in the China Club, but she is not a girlfriend of his. *I* am his girlfriend. In this past year that I've been sick, Kelsey's only been out twice. Kelsey's a great guy to me—but he just screwed up. That's all it was. He made a mistake. We all make mistakes, don't we?"

She continued to be his staunchest defender. She also refused to hear that he had continued his party-hardy ways even after having been arrested the second time. To this day she claims Kelsey was clean and sober their last two years together—a claim many others would dispute.

While his friends and attorney spent considerable time and energy making a lot of excuses for Kelsey's failure to comply, a more probable reason lies simply in the powerful lure of cocaine. One of the many effects of the drug is its ability to become the overriding priority in the user's life. Daily appointments and responsibilities get put on the back burner because the primary goal is to stay high. At the same time the brain feels turned on, it also loses its ability to concentrate. And any feelings of remorse that might be felt over squandering one's time—not to mention money—can be quickly cured by doing another line.

Kelsey ended up being released after "just" ten days in the county slammer. The short-term effect of his confinement was a renewed sense of follow-through. By the last week in July, Grammer had finished his highway clean-up stint and was steadying himself for the hearing on his cocaine charge, which was scheduled for the first week in August.

On August 6 Grammer pleaded no contest to the charge of cocaine possession, then held his breath. According to a sentencing report prepared by the court, Grammer admitted to "extensive use" of alcohol since age nine, using cocaine since 1979, and experimenting with Valium, Ecstasy, and marijuana. The report went on to say that Grammer turned to drugs to escape reality, then outlined the family tragedies Kelsey had endured.

This time around, the court was more lenient. Kelsey was sentenced to ninety days of house arrest, three years of probation, and a $500 fine. He was also ordered to attend a drug abuse treatment program and to perform three hundred more hours of community service—this time not with Caltrans, however.

The term of his house arrest extended past the day when the 1990 Emmy Awards would be given out. Kelsey had been nominated for Best Supporting Actor, and he felt he had a good chance to win, but it was hardly a time to quibble with the court. Leaving the courthouse, Kelsey joked that he could always prerecord an acceptance speech.

Grammer must have let out a sigh of relief. Under the provisions of the house arrest, Kelsey was able to go to work as long as he wore an electronic device on his wrist or ankle that allowed authorities to monitor his whereabouts. As it turned out, his probation officer allowed Grammer to attend the Emmys, although he didn't win. But considering that he still had his freedom, still had his fiancée, and still had a job, Kelsey must have felt like a winner.

Once again the worst seemed behind him. But the seductive pull of cocaine would prove impossible for Kelsey to resist.

On November 8, 1990, the *Cheers* cast flew to Boston to celebrate the show's two hundredth episode. Beantown rolled out the welcome mat and threw the stars a huge celebration complete with parade. For all the cast members, it should have been a day of accomplishment and gaiety. But for Kelsey, it also meant facing fans after a difficult year full of legal and personal problems. The same man who claimed to feel most at home on a stage in front of a live audience was terrified to face the crowd lining the streets outside. The obvious difference was that onstage Kelsey adopted another character, while in real life he had to stand and face the masses as himself.

Like a battered spouse running back to an abusive husband, Kelsey returned to cocaine. That way, in case he was booed, the pain would be numbed. According to published reports, Grammer snorted the drug in his hotel before braving the crush of fans lining the street waiting for the parade.

"Kelsey was acting like a madman," said one spectator at the time. "He was flipping his earmuffs off his head even though it was freezing cold outside. But everyone just assumed he was being fun old Kelsey, having a good time."

Flushed with what the other revelers thought was excitement instead of a cocaine rush, Grammer addressed the crowd: "I know now why Frasier makes such a good living in this town. You're all suffering from mass psychosis."

Interestingly, nobody in the *Cheers* cast suspected Kelsey had slipped until he told them. But first he admitted his drug use to his probation officer. Luckily Grammer wasn't tossed in jail for violating parole, but Van Nuys Superior Court Judge James Coleman added two additional years of probation onto Kelsey's current sentence, and ordered him to undergo regular drug testing.

Los Angeles district attorney Teri Hutchinson commented on Grammer's lapse. "If he continues his drug use, his probation will probably be terminated and he will be sentenced to either a county jail or state prison.

"If he shows no further signs of drug and alcohol abuse and completes his sentence, his probation will be finished in August 1995."

By the end of 1990, Grammer felt as if he'd been through a meat grinder. He particularly resented the intense media interest in his court dramas.

"The tabloids had a field day," Kelsey says, referring to the coverage. "They said I was on suicide watch. But it was the first time in ten years I didn't have to worry about anything and [could] get some sleep. I'll admit I'd been running from the problem—I tried to negotiate it away instead of facing up. But I've been clean and honest. I may have a drink now and then, but that's it."

But as with everything else about Kelsey, that wasn't just it.

FIVE

Kelsey rang in the new year of 1991 with some much-needed resolutions. He had to keep his nose clean—literally and figuratively. And he needed to be smarter, since there would be no more second chances. One more slip-up and he could kiss his job—and freedom—good-bye. Some of the solutions were simple: Instead of driving himself or going with friends, for example, he began to hire a limo when he went bar- and club-hopping. He had more than enough money, and it was a rather practical solution, allowing him to drink without having to worry about a DUI. And despite all that had happened, Kelsey was still a devoted drinker.

Kelsey also found comfort in work, which provided a creative sanctuary that offered some measure of balance in a life so startlingly out of kilter. His profile on the show had grown continually as Frasier became a more and more central character, in no small part because of Frasier's marriage to the equally debonair and tasteful Lilith, played by Bebe Neuwirth. Their on-screen relationship transfused new blood into the long-running series—although their offscreen compatibility reportedly deteriorated over the years and may have played a part in Neuwirth's decision to leave the show.

But in early 1991 things were smooth, on camera and off, with Grammer and Neuwirth engaging in flirtatious banter during interviews, playing up the sexual chemistry between Frasier and Lilith.

"The best thing about Lilith is her ass," Kelsey said while looking pointedly at Bebe.

"No, no—not about me," Neuwirth protested.

"But it's all in the same package!"

"They have a good marriage," Kelsey observed about their TV alter egos. "After all, Frasier is *hot* for Lilith. And he's a romantic sort of chap. For Valentine's Day, he would take Lilith on a trip to the islands . . . with a suitcase full of sex toys."

"Right," laughed Neuwirth. "He'd bring this huge trunk and tell people all he had was his toothbrush. Actually, if I have any complaints about some of the scripts, it's that we haven't been able to manifest that heat."

"Yeah," Grammer said. "Frasier and Lilith have sex *all* the time."

And so, apparently, did Kelsey—and not just with his girlfriend of the moment.

Fidelity was not one of Kelsey's strengths—or top priorities, for that matter. Throughout his relationship with Cerlette, Grammer had a roving eye and a libido in constant overdrive. Displaying little-boy vulnerability combined with old-school gentility,

Kelsey made the ladies swoon. His status as a TV star certainly didn't hurt, either.

"Kelsey had groupies," says a friend simply. "Who didn't? We all did. One time we all went out with Kelsey and a few others—Cerlette stayed home. Kelsey and another person had taken a limo. We partied and drank heavily, and I was getting ready to leave, but we couldn't find Kelsey anywhere. We knew he couldn't have left because the limo was still parked outside. Finally one of the friends with us opened the door of the limo, and there was Kelsey, having sex with some girl he had just met at the bar.

"My friend said, 'Hey, Kelsey, aren't you going to invite us in?'

"Kelsey told us they were just finishing up. In a little while he came back into the bar, grabbed another drink, and said, 'You saved me just in time. I couldn't get rid of her. I told her I had to take you guys home.'"

But as a rule, Kelsey's entanglements with women were rarely resolved that neatly. In fact, his relationships with women were often a lightning rod for the major problems in his life. But he never seemed to learn.

"Women have messed Kelsey up," a friend says with blind loyalty, and with what some might consider to be more than a little bit of misdirected misogyny.

"They've been such a thorn in his side, there were times he didn't feel like going on. He's been known to say, 'This is bullshit—everything I've got goes to alimony and support payments.'

"He always thought if he could find the right girl,

he'd be more content and not always out there aimlessly searching. He'd settle down and get more focused about what would make him happy in life.

"His friends would always tell him the problem was he picked up too much baggage. We told him to get rid of the baggage. It's a financial drain, all this baggage. We joke that his dick cost him more money than anything else—and it's true. He likes to entertain the ladies."

Entertaining the ladies was more than a hobby; it was an obsessive pursuit during his rise to stardom on *Cheers*. Ironically, on the series Frasier finds his soul mate in Lilith, the woman who makes him whole. But offscreen a parade of women marched into—and out of—his life with revolving-door regularity. Kelsey's friends watched helplessly as he immersed himself in a lifestyle he thought would make him happy. But the bevy of babes and constantly living the good life with its continual partying only seemed to make Kelsey more desolate in moments of sobriety. Which is probably why those moments were few and far between.

His friends watched as Kelsey forged romantic links with women who brought him more pain than joy.

"We've all been critical of the girls he brings around," the friend says, singing a familiar tune. "We would all stand around looking at each other, saying, 'Where the fuck did this one come from?' It's just a physical thing with most of them.

"You know, the very girl he attracts to himself is the very girl he will end up resenting and despising. Still, those are the ones who go out and have such a fun time with him."

Through it all, Lamme remained almost slavishly devoted to Kelsey.

"It was like she was addicted to Kelsey," observed a friend of the couple. "She would show up on the set nearly every day, like being with Kelsey was her purpose in life. Between takes or when there was a break from rehearsal, she'd run over and be all over him. It was kind of embarrassing."

Maybe it was just a case of clinging more tightly to something she was afraid of losing. And Cerlette was indeed on verge of losing him, whether she wanted to admit it to herself or not.

In the spring of 1991, Kelsey learned he was going to be a father for the second time—except the happy mom-to-be was not longtime girlfriend Cerlette Lamme. It was Cerlette's best friend, a makeup artist named Barrie Buckner.

It was a cruel blow to the woman who had waged a one-person pro-Kelsey campaign. Previously, when biting tabloid stories appeared detailing his infidelities, Cerlette spoke out, insisting he was loyal to her. Little did she know that in addition to countless one-night stands and flavors-of-the-month, Grammer was carrying on a secret two-year affair with her best friend.

In a pathetic irony, Cerlette had actually wanted to hook Barrie up with Kelsey's hard-partying *Cheers* buddy Woody Harrelson. She had fixated on the idea that Barrie would be perfect for Woody, so she and Kelsey arranged to go on a double date with them. Lamme was making a match, all right, but not the one she expected.

After the double date, Harrelson and Buckner dutifully went out together a few times, but they soon stopped dating, claiming there were no sparks. But as it turned out, there was plenty of heat between Barrie and Kelsey.

"One night when Cerlette was out of town, Kelsey threw a party on his boat, which is docked in Marina Del Rey," recalls a friend who was at the party. "He invited about ten people—including Barrie. He spent most of the night talking to her, and by the end of the evening they were in each other's arms."

And Buckner was soon in Grammer's bed.

Always careful not to get caught, Kelsey continued his affair with Buckner on and off for two years. Often they rendezvoused back in the marina on Kelsey's boat, the gentle slap of water against the hull providing romantic sound effects.

In fact, Grammer's relationship with Cerlette had probably already begun its slow, painful demise even before Buckner entered the picture. But neither seemed able to be the one to walk away—and stay away. In 1991 Cerlette moved out of the run-down San Fernando Valley house where she had lived with Kelsey for years and into her own place—although within a short time she was back spending most of her time over at Fort Grammer.

Most thought the news that Barrie was carrying Kelsey's child would finally be the straw that broke the camel's back. They assumed it would be impossible to fix the damage that affair had done to Cerlette. Not even the smooth-talking actor who had apologized to a policeman for not admitting he was carrying cocaine in his pocket would be able to talk his way out of this one. And most thought he wouldn't necessarily want to, either.

But, surprisingly, this revelation was not the end of things between them. Even after suffering the pain and humiliation of having the world know that Kelsey had been having an affair behind her back with her best friend, who was now pregnant with his baby, Cerlette was unable to make a clean break with Kelsey. Somehow Cerlette weathered this storm and kept desperately trying to hold it all together, even though it was obvious to others that their relationship was already cracking under the weight of Kelsey's drug use, heavy drinking, and chronic infidelity.

To some, it smacked of masochism. To others who knew Lamme, it was testimony to the depth of her love.

Among their friends there were also differences in the amount of sympathy for Cerlette. Some thought a breakup was way overdue, believing Cerlette an "enabler" who did nothing to help Kelsey quit the booze and drugs. Others thought she was a loyal lover who deserved better.

The news of Kelsey's pending fatherhood hit the papers in October, bringing another wave of intense media scrutiny and curious looks from coworkers. Most people couldn't complicate their lives this much if they tried, but for Kelsey, it was a regular occurrence. What would he do for an encore?

Throughout his life, when the pressures of his private life seemed ready to erupt, his art came to the rescue and offered Kelsey sanctuary. This time was no exception. In April of 1992 Grammer returned to the stage. It couldn't have come at a better time professionally, too. Although he enjoyed his working environment on *Cheers*, he was feeling antsy.

"He was frustrated," says one friend. "He couldn't get any feature film work, and none of the outside work that he wanted panned out. In a sense, he felt locked into the character of Dr. Frasier Crane. Back then, though, I think a lot of people were afraid to hire him because of his deserved reputation as a hard, hard partier. His acting itself was never compromised, so it wasn't that. On-screen, his talent shows that.

"But he was bored for a while on *Cheers* and was even considering leaving the show. Which is ironic, considering how close he had come to being booted off. He talked to some of the other cast members who were also worried about being typecast—a lot of people who come off a long-running series never work again. Kelsey had that fear.

"After he 'made it' on *Cheers*, his career seemed to stagnate. But then again, he didn't really try anymore because he didn't have to. His struggling days were over. He thought, 'OK, I've peaked at this plateau—but what next?' He was real insecure about what his future held, and he went through a period of depression, really searching for what else there is in life."

Relief came in the form of Shakespeare, so it was back to the boards and the Bard. And back to the Mark Taper Forum, where he had appeared in *Measure for Measure* and where he had met Cerlette. The sense of having come full circle could not have escaped Grammer. But so much had changed since his initial appearance at the Taper. In that first play, Kelsey was a secondary character, but this time around he had the starring role in *Richard II*.

It was a homecoming long overdue. Over the past few years, Kelsey had become too consumed by drinking and drugs to pursue as much theater work as he would have otherwise. At times it was all he could do to drag himself to the set. So instead, the theater came looking for Kelsey. He came into the production a week and a half after John Glover, who had originally been cast in the title role, left to fulfill a TV contract. Shakespeare's complicated king was an ironically appropriate role for Grammer, who describes Richard II this way:

"In the first act, he's a power-mad egomaniac. Then, because of his dethroning, he discovers his humanity and becomes a human being. As he descends in terms of power, there's an ascendancy of his humanity and self-discovery, which is what makes him tragic in the end. The role makes you take a look at your mortality and belief system."

If he was looking objectively, Grammer could not have liked what he saw. But as was the case throughout Grammer's adult life, few around him ever seemed to grasp the turmoil beneath the surface. All they saw was a charming chap with tons of talent.

"Kelsey's the last—at least in my lifetime—of the inspired, irreverent people," said Robert Egan, who directed *Richard II* and who worked with Kelsey in *Measure for Measure*. "He's got a wild streak in him. He's managed to retain the inspired child, which most people approaching forty say good-bye to. He's a powerful, primitive man. He knows what suffering is about. He's intelligent and gifted at language."

But sadly deficient as a grown-up—and as a judge of what he needed.

April of 1992 would be a significant time for another reason. It was during April that Kelsey met a woman who would throw his life into more turmoil than even he could imagine. Together, they would nearly destroy each other—which some would say seemed to be exactly what Kelsey was searching for. This was a man who many felt desperately needed therapy, and that is what his next relationship would finally drive him to.

Grammer's love affair and marriage to Leigh-Ann Csuhany would turn out to be one of the most violent, outrageous, sick relationships ever played out painfully in public view, even by Hollywood's often seamy standards.

However, in the spring of 1992, he was simply a man in love with a twenty-two-year-old exotic dancer—or in layman's terms, a stripper. Of course, he didn't care what Csuhany did for a living when he spotted her at a San Fernando Valley restaurant. Leigh-Ann stole his heart quickly, and Kelsey was a willing victim. At the beginning of their affair, Kelsey stayed true to form, preferring to juggle several women, including Cerlette, rather than make a commitment to any one person.

Making a commitment to Barrie had never been a consideration, though. When she stunned Kelsey with the news that she was pregnant, his first reaction had been to try to make it go away by telling Buckner he didn't want to get married, or even to settle down with her and raise the child together.

However, having already gone through the wringer once over child support with his first wife, Kelsey did not want to get embroiled in a nasty, public dispute about child support, so he assured Barrie he would be financially responsible. But there was a hitch.

"Barrie had to sign an agreement promising not to ever talk about her relationship with Kelsey," says an acquaintance. "It's your basic gag order. If Barrie wants Kelsey to keep writing the checks, she had better keep her mouth shut."

Part of Grammer's sensitivity can be traced to the intense scrutiny he suffered at the hands of the press, in particular the tabloid press, during his legal problems earlier in the year. The last thing he wanted was to have the tabloids get their hands on another juicy scandal. Even though he knew they would run the story, at least this way he wouldn't have to read comments from Buckner about their affair.

And after years of putting it off, Kelsey was about to make the final break from Cerlette, too. Ironically, the very people who complained loudest about Cerlette would be howling objections about the woman who replaced her.

After seven years and a lifetime's worth of tough times, Cerlette and Kelsey split up for good after he confessed to Lamme that he had fallen in love with another woman. To her credit, Cerlette took it with amazing good grace. And to Kelsey's relief, she didn't immediately run to the nearest tabloid and sell a tell-all about her years with him. To the end, she remained true blue.

"Cerlette was a great chick, a great gal," says

Bobby Diamond, who also once dated her. "She and Kelsey got along good but ended badly. She was very straight and very honest."

Which is more than can be said for Grammer, who, despite Cerlette's numerous public proclamations, had found it nearly impossible to be monogamous during his years with Lamme. On the other side, friends defend Kelsey's roving eye by saying that deep in his heart he knew Cerlette wasn't the one he was looking to settle down with for good, that she didn't offer him the kind of anchoring stability he needed. The signs had been there for years that their relationship would ultimately end on a sour note.

Their notoriously pigstylike Van Nuys house served as a kind of analogy to their relationship—a mirror of the chaos that was Kelsey's internal life, says one close friend. While Cerlette might not have been the center of the storm, she was certainly caught in its swirl.

"Kelsey was always fighting with Cerlette," recalls a frequent house guest. "I heard him tell her, 'Get the fuck out—I can't stand you. I don't want to be with you.' And she'd scream back—they'd go at it pretty good."

In what appears to be a trend, Grammer's friends by and large didn't care much for Lamme—or any of his other girlfriends, for that matter.

"It wasn't like his friends embraced her as a nice person—nobody really cared for her," says a friend. "They just tolerated her and were nice to her because she was his girlfriend. But we all felt her insecurities made her cling to Kelsey's fame and fortune. It didn't come across as a healthy relationship—she seemed totally into his fame trip. But I think the reason he stayed with her for so long was because she was real supportive of him. He needed that feeling of emotional support from her. But let's face it, if he was still the great, funny character he is now but worked at a local gas station pumping gas instead of being a TV star, she wouldn't have been hanging out with him."

A year after, Cerlette was finally able to admit what everyone had long known. "I couldn't take the cheating."

That's the most damning thing she's ever said against Grammer. And despite being urged to do so by lawyers, Lamme also declined to try to wrangle any palimony out of Grammer, even though they were together seven years. She did talk about it once, though, to the ire of Kelsey's friends.

"We told her she wasn't even his wife," says a friend. "She was just his girlfriend. Yeah, they lived together seven years, but they never even had kids."

Cerlette's comment about palimony, which was possibly offhand or spurred by the pain she was feeling, confirmed a belief Kelsey had long held: that nearly all women were out to become involved with him just to get his money. Maybe he forgot that when Cerlette fell in love with him, he was a temporarily transplanted New York stage actor who intended to be in California only six weeks.

"But Kelsey became fixated on [the idea of] women using him," his friend explains. "His attitude really was, 'I can date you for two years, we can break up tomorrow, and you're already looking for money out of me.'

"The reason he had a hard time finding security with any girl is that his guard was always up. He just *knew* people were after his money because our society promotes materialism rather than love.

"Kelsey mentioned this right after he broke it off with Cerlette. He said, 'It's amazing how we break up and she goes right for the money.' He was feeling anger toward people who seem genuine with their fake smiles and then when the going gets tough, they're out to get you. You know, sign on the dotted line. That's the stuff that really angered him."

Not that Kelsey was strapped for cash. Earning money turned out to be a far simpler pursuit than finding the true love many of his friends believed he yearned for. Despite its longevity, *Cheers* was still a top-ten show. While Kelsey didn't make the money Ted Danson did—Danson was the highest-paid sitcom star in the history of television, with a salary in excess of $15 million—Grammer was still raking in several million a year during the last couple of seasons.

But his bank account balance did nothing to ease Kelsey's concern over people wanting his money. The friend says that Kelsey still had a bee in his bonnet about Doreen all these years later.

"Kelsey was very, very bitter with her because he felt Doreen tried to take him for everything."

Grammer's tunnel vision is interesting. In his mind's eye he is the victim. Maybe most telling is a comment he made during an interview in 1993, a variation of a theme he had voiced to friends many times before.

"I tend to fall into relationships with people who

are very needy and difficult to please. That pattern is familiar to me as what love is. My grandmother, my mother, and my sister were very demanding. After my grandfather died, I assumed the burden of trying to take care of three women who were impossible to please. I expected people to be happy because of my efforts—and nobody was. So I get wrapped up in people like that.

"I admire people who aren't as controlled as I am. If I could actually release my emotions the way I'd like to in real life, I'd have been in jail a long time ago."

But in 1992, Kelsey wasn't thinking about how his past was affecting his present, nor about lessons he should have learned. He wasn't wasting time on introspection to figure out why his relationships all ended so badly. Kelsey was too busy being in love.

With Cerlette out of the picture, he was free to pursue Leigh-Ann as passionately as he wanted, and to start telling people about the wonderful woman he had found. But one thing did give him pause—Leigh-Ann's "career." Not that he cared, but he just knew how the tabloids would sink their teeth into that one. Still gun-shy of any negative publicity, Grammer was determined to do whatever he could to keep Leigh-Ann's former profession—or for that matter, even the details of how they met—out of the hands of the prying press.

When asked, Kelsey simply sidestepped the issue.

"A bar—that's all I'm going to say. But you could say it's a place we both like to go."

Grammer had been a celebrity long enough to know that displaying that kind of coyness was like throwing down a gauntlet in front of the press. If

Kelsey didn't want to say, then he must have something to hide, the reasoning went; and the search to ferret out the real Leigh-Ann Csuhany was on. It was only a matter of time before they retraced her steps or someone volunteered the information. And sure enough, that's exactly what happened.

SIX

If Kelsey hated the tabloids before, he must have been gnashing his teeth when Leigh-Ann's "secret life" as a stripper was revealed in an August 1992 *Star* article. The story spared no details on Csuhany's gyrating work, including a stint at the Gotham City strip club in Los Angeles.

"None of us could believe it when he walked in," another of the club's dancers commented on a night Kelsey spent at the club a while after he had met Leigh-Ann. "We were all whispering among ourselves, wondering if it really was the *Cheers* guy. But Leigh-Ann walked straight over to him."

Csuhany, a 5'3" twenty-two-year-old who weighed in at a curvy 120 pounds, made sure Kelsey had a good time.

"She was positively swooning all over him," the dancer recalls. "She was cupping his head in her hands and stroking his beard."

That night, which was prior to the *Star*'s blowing

the whistle on Leigh-Ann's being a stripper,
Grammer was in such high spirits he even auto-
graphed copies of the *Star* for some fans. It was an
issue that featured a picture of him and Csuhany
on the cover. In it Leigh-Ann was carrying the
same little purple makeup case she actually used at
the club.

Kelsey had no problem patronizing the club and,
thanks to that patronage, was able to get management to agree to his adamant insistence that this
part of his life with Leigh-Ann be kept confidential.
A gag order was imposed on everyone—which in
turn irritated enough people to the point of actually
inspiring them to talk.

"Kelsey insisted that if anyone asked us, we deny
that she ever worked here," says a dancer. "Kelsey
told me that it wouldn't be cool for his career if her
background got out. He also told me he'd be the
laughingstock of the *Cheers* set if his costars found
out about her career as a dancer."

On its surface, this seems like a disingenuous
concern, considering the antics that regularly
occurred on the set of *Cheers*.

"It was like a locker room," says former extra
Elizabeth Roy. "As a woman, a lot of times it was
hard not to feel like a piece of meat—and the producers tended to just ignore it. There'd often be
questions directed at female extras about what kind
of underwear they were wearing or if they were
wearing a bra or not.

"One of the boys' favorite things was when they
hired several models to come to the set for the
afternoon—and pay them more money than the
extras were getting. These girls would come in

wearing low-cut, ultra-tight tops and skin-tight skirts. And of course they'd all be very big-busted.

"The girls would hang around for the afternoon flirting with the guys—John Ratzenberger, Ted Danson, George Wendt, and Kelsey. The talk would be raunchy, with a lot of double entendres and innuendo. It was pretty disgusting watching all these grown men acting like adolescent high-school boys."

"It's true, the men on that show acted like a bunch of eighth graders," says one of the show's writers. "It wasn't unusual on the show for the writers to write in an encounter for Ted's character with some bimbo. Inevitably Kelsey would hit on the woman playing the bimbo.

"It's funny—on camera it would be Ted's character chasing after the bimbo like a dog in heat, but behind the scenes it was Kelsey sniffing around. It's as if he were acting out Sam Malone in real life.

"But Kelsey coming on was hardly anything new. In fact, one time he came on to a woman who was very much with another cast member. They were at a party and after a couple of drinks [he] came over and seductively slipped his arm around her waist. She knew all about Kelsey and her reaction was like, 'Oh, God, here we go. The guy's a little drunk and using it as an excuse to make a pass.'

"She very politely stepped away, and that was the end of that. And of course she never said anything to Kelsey's castmate because he would have wanted to rip Kelsey in two—although I'm sure Kelsey would have assured him the lady was simply mistaken and very well may have talked his way out of it.

"But these were the kinds of things that people around Kelsey were too familiar with—but that nobody watching the show at home ever suspected."

There were a lot of things that fans never suspected about the man who played Frasier Crane. For one thing, Kelsey was surprisingly superstitious, considering his formidable intellect. One of his most peculiar quirks, which he still has to this day, concerns his car keys.

"Before Kelsey goes onstage for a performance, he's got to have his car keys in his back pocket," says the writer. "It goes back to the insecurities all actors feel to a degree before getting in front of an audience, whether it be stage or television. In his mind, Kelsey knows that if he ever does a terrible job, or if people really hate him, he can walk off the set and immediately leave without having to go back to his dressing room. Not too dissimilar from when David Caruso filmed his last scene on *NYPD Blue* and walked off the set and out the door, never to return.

"Except in Kelsey's case, it's merely a safety net of escape—not that he thinks he'd ever actually do such a thing. He's no David Caruso. But those keys are always there, and you can see him patting his back pocket just before he makes an entrance."

For all the publicity about his court problems, what the fans also didn't know was how many close calls Kelsey had had with the law. Some of the incidents could have landed him in more hot water.

"One time, Kelsey was back East, taking a long trip on his boat," recalls the writer. "He had been out sailing in international waters and was on his

Frasier checks pregnant wife Dr. Lilith Stenin in the 1988 *Cheers* episode "How to Win Friends and Electrocute People." (© AP/Wide World)

The cast and crew of *Cheers* celebrates the show's 200th episode. *Back row, from the left:* John Ratzenberger, Rhea Perlman, Roger Rees, Kirstie Alley, Ted Danson, Woody Harrelson, Shelley Long, George Wendt. *Front row:* Kelsey and Bebe Neuwirth. (© AP/Wide World)

On location in Boston for *Cheers* in 1993, the cast
tapes the *Tonight Show* at the Bull & Finch Pub.
From the left: Woody Harrelson, John Ratzenberger,
Kelsey, Rhea Perlman, and Ted Danson.
(© AP/Wide World)

Outside the pub with Jay Leno. (© AP/Wide World)

May 20, 1993, was declared *Cheers* day in Massachusetts. Here, cast members address a crowd at the Statehouse. (© AP/Wide World)

A low point: On May 10, 1990, Kelsey turned himself in to authorities in Van Nuys, CA, in response to arrest warrants issued for skipping court dates. (© AP/Wide World)

Toothbrush in pocket, Kelsey sits in Van Nuys Municipal Court on May 24, 1990. He had surrendered to begin serving a thirty-day sentence for a probation violation, stemming from his 1987 drunken driving conviction.
(© AP/Wide World)

From bad to worse: While serving his thirty-day sentence, Kelsey sits in Van Nuys Municipal Court on May 30, 1990, where he was ordered to stand trial on a felony drug charge.
(© AP/Wide World)

August 6, 1990; surrounded by the press, Kelsey enters Superior Court in Van Nuys to plead no contest to a felony cocaine possession charge. He was placed under house arrest for ninety days and ordered to wear an electronic surveillance device so authorities could monitor his movements.
(© AP/Wide World)

Kelsey at the 20th Annual People's Choice Awards on March 8, 1994, holding the award he won for favorite male performer in a new TV series.
(© AP/Wide World)

Kelsey and Cerlette Lamme at the Toyota Grand Prix in April 1989. (©1994 by Scott Down/Celebrity Photo)

Kelsey and wife Leigh-Ann Csuhany, in 1991, during their brief marriage. (©1994 by Janet Gough/Celebrity Photo)

Kelsey and Candice Bergen, star of *Murphy Brown*, celebrate their 1994 Emmy wins. (© AP/Wide World)

The cast of *Frasier* holds their 1994 Emmy awards. (© AP/Wide World)

Kelsey and Tammi Baliszewski arrive at the 46th Primetime Emmy Awards on September 11, 1994. (© AP/Wide World)

way back into American waters very late at night when he was stopped by a Coast Guard cutter. The Coast Guard patrols the water and one of their primary jobs is to look for drug smugglers. A lot of the cocaine that's brought into this country is smuggled in by boat.

"And of course Kelsey is carrying a small amount of cocaine for his personal use. He panics when he sees that the Guard is going to board his boat with drug-sniffing dogs. He knows what they're really looking for is pounds of powder, but the dogs will smell what he has on him just as easily.

"Luckily for him, Kelsey managed to toss his vial overboard without being seen. He said afterward, though, that he was pissed off because it was the last coke he had."

Imagine the field day the press would have had with that one—"Grammer Busted by Coast Guard." But the fact that it never happened was small consolation for Kelsey, who felt his private life had been dissected enough. And in the case of his new love, he was determined to do what he could to keep their privacy intact. At his urging, Csuhany quit Gotham City in May. It didn't take much arm-twisting. The deal was simple—he was going to take care of her so she didn't need to work there anymore. Csuhany saw her position with Kelsey solidifying, and looked forward to being a lady of leisure.

"Leigh-Ann quit in a heartbeat," the dancer says. "She told us that Kelsey had promised to marry her."

And to prove she wasn't just blowing hot air, Leigh-Ann couldn't resist coming back later to show off her four-carat engagement ring—a tanzanite surrounded by diamond clusters.

Leigh-Ann remembers the day Kelsey proposed and speaks wistfully about his romantic side.

"I was really mad at him that day, bitching at him left and right. All of a sudden, at about three o'clock in the afternoon, he asked me to come outside. I had no idea why he'd want me outside. In front of the house we lived at in Agoura Hills are these big pillars you can sit on. He plopped me down and said, 'Close your eyes.'

"Like I said, I was in a bitchy mood and said something like, 'What do you want? What's going on?' But he just said 'Close your eyes' again, so I did.

"On my marriage finger I wore a diamond ring. It was an engagement ring that I got from a guy when I was fifteen and I had always kept it. He took off the ring and all I felt was him slip something on my finger. My first thought was that he was going to propose to me with my own ring! So I opened my eyes and there was a big fat blue tanzanite sitting on my finger.

"He was on one knee and said, 'I'm giving you this because I was blue before I met you, and blue in the Japanese culture is the meaning of spring and spring is the beginning of new life.' Those were his exact words. And then he asked me to be his wife. I cried and gave him a big hug and kiss and said yes.

"We had an appointment to go to Griffith Observatory that weekend because his friend is the manager there and we got to go at twelve-thirty at night, after it was closed, to see the stars. About a week later he told me he had planned to propose to me there underneath the stars, but he couldn't wait because the ring was burning a hole in his pocket.

"A while before he asked me to marry him, Kelsey and I had talked about what we wanted in life. I said I wanted to get married, I wanted to have a husband, and I wanted to have kids. He had said he didn't want to get married again because he had had such a brutal divorce from Doreen."

But Kelsey had changed his mind, much to Leigh-Ann's joy. Csuhany admitted to her old dancing pals she was anxious to get married, but that Kelsey wanted to wait until he was done with the season. But it wasn't just a ploy to put her off. Grammer really did intend to marry her and was so slaphappy about it, he even talked to one of the hated tabloids about his engagement.

"We have six dogs—Leigh-Ann loves dogs. She's a very understanding woman. I've never been happier—Leigh Anne is the one I've been waiting for."

And boy, was he going to get it.

Which is exactly what his friends were afraid of. It was alarmingly clear where Kelsey's relationship with Leigh-Ann was heading. They had seen it all before—Kelsey falling for the wrong woman. And as he always did, Kelsey brought the woman around to meet and hang out with his friends. Always polite, the friends would be cordial, but in private they would shake their heads and say to each other, "Kelsey's gone and done it again."

But Leigh-Ann was the one all agreed proved Kelsey had gone too far—maybe too far ever to come back. Marriage seemed inevitable.

His life with Csuhany was beginning to take an obvious toll, both at home and on the set. Bebe Neuwirth, whose Lilith character had helped establish *Frasier* as a major player, announced she was leaving the show. The official reason was that she wanted to pursue feature film roles, which was no doubt true. But at least one friend of the actress says her frustration with Kelsey might have hurried her departure.

"Basically, Bebe just despised the fact that she had to do every scene with Kelsey," says the writer. "Bebe was never one of the inner circle on *Cheers*. Maybe she thought she was more of a serious actress because of her film roles, who knows? But Kelsey was just not her favorite person. You never saw Bebe running down to the jailhouse to cheer Kelsey up. She was glad to be going."

"Bebe's just tired of working with him," said a person at the time. "She's had enough—she doesn't have to or want to put up with his behavior. Bebe showed Kelsey a lot of compassion and patience when he was going through all his legal problems. But things have gone downhill recently. He comes to work late, unrested, unshaved, and looking like some bum off the street.

"Bebe thinks the change in Kelsey has to do with Leigh-Ann, but her tolerance has run out. She's on the verge of having a major clash with him but is loath to do anything to cause disruption before she leaves. Bebe just keeps telling herself she only has a few more episodes and to keep it together.

"But at the same time she has asked for some concessions from the producers—and they've agreed. Bebe is now allowed to arrive up to an hour late on tape day since Kelsey is regularly that late, too. Bebe didn't think it was fair that she had to sit around waiting for him.

"It's not just Bebe—all the cast members are extremely worried about Kelsey. It's just that her tolerance has run out and theirs hasn't."

The general consensus was that Leigh-Ann was behind the most recent change in Kelsey. This was an evaluation his friends couldn't agree more with.

"We couldn't stand her," admits a close friend of Grammer. "We saw clearly what she was about—she was moving in for the kill. To be honest, we all wanted Kelsey to get rid of her, but she orchestrated the relationship perfectly and ended up moving in. Leigh-Ann tried to completely take over Kelsey's life. Our running joke was that she must be the best Kelsey's ever had in bed, because what else could make a man so blind?

"To me, she was just so gross. Her appearance, her mannerisms, her disposition were always tacky and slutty. Everyone was worried—even Woody Harrelson tried to talk to him. All his friends tried to say something, but it fell on deaf ears. We all wondered what had happened—where did we go wrong with Kelsey? Somebody wake *us* up from this nightmare."

Not all of Grammer's friends tried to interfere, but Leigh-Ann was so objectionable, so offensive, so *obvious* that even the most diplomatic were unable to hold their tongues.

"I remember around the time of the last episode of *Cheers*, Kelsey was with Leigh-Ann. We were playing football on the set and I was joking with him, but there's always truth in sarcasm. I was ribbing him about Leigh-Ann's background. Kelsey and I were close enough, so finally I said to him, 'What am I missing? What don't I see in Leigh-Ann that attracts you so much to her?'

"He made some kind of sexual joke as a come-back—that was his answer. A couple of people standing nearby turned their heads and coughed uncomfortably because it was so unpleasant when he brought Leigh-Ann around. Everyone on the set could see what she was about—she was a typical gold digger."

But all Kelsey saw was a red-haired firebrand. He didn't see her coarseness. And despite his constant grumbling and complaining about women only wanting to be with him because of his money, he chose the very woman his friends all believed was only out to get what she could.

Except Kelsey didn't care what his friends or anybody else thought. But then again, nobody likes to be told they're being a fool—or being made a fool of. The more you tell someone not to do some-thing, the greater the odds they will. It's simple human nature. But Grammer's choice nearly destroyed both of them.

As always, there's another side to the story—Leigh-Ann's side. She says she definitely felt the sting of rejection from his friends, and is familiar with the gold-digger accusations.

"But I didn't twist his arm! I didn't force him over to the jeweler's."

And from where she stood, it was really Kelsey's friends who were the ones long taking advantage of him.

"I met Kelsey at the Pelican's Retreat, a restaurant in Calabasas," Csuhany remembers. "I was in town from Canada visiting my sister. It was a Sunday and they had rock and roll night. Two of his friends were trying to pick me up using Kelsey's name. It was not cute—I told one of the guys to blow it out his ass. These were just a couple of his leech friends who would hang out with him—going out in the limo with him, squeezing money out of him.

"I looked over at Kelsey and he looked at me. I knew who he was but turned around and walked away and I pretended I didn't know who he was. Twenty minutes later he came up to me and apologized for his friends and formally introduced himself. So I introduced myself back—but I still pretended I'd never heard of Kelsey Grammer, let alone *Cheers*.

"He asked me to go with him to another bar for a cocktail, and I accepted. It was the Red Onion in Thousand Oaks.

"First I went to my car and locked it, then we hopped into the limo. I'm not the type to just hop into someone's car, but I went with him because of *who* he was. I wouldn't hop into even a limo if I didn't know the person.

"After the Red Onion, he asked me to go to his house for a drink and I told him I wanted to pick my car up first. So we went back to the Pelican so I could get my car. I drove to his house and we drank until seven in the morning but nothing happened—I went home. We exchanged phone numbers but I never called him. He called me and chased me for about three weeks."

Leigh-Ann remembers it as a giddy time and

loved every minute of attention he showered on her.

"He left me really nice messages on my machine—messages that said he wanted to take me out on a date. Yeah, he's a romantic, I'll have to give him that. He knows how to blind people!" She laughs loudly before continuing with her recollections of how she and Kelsey fell in love.

"Finally I went out with him. I accepted a date and we went to a wonderful French restaurant in Encino and had a really great meal. I was wined and dined and then went back to his place, spent the night, and started dating him. And I guess the rest is history.

"He was sweet. I remember the first thing that was really cool, the one thing I really liked is that he had a lot of respect. I was used to long-haired rock-and-rollers, bum musicians. The first date, the thing that stuck in my mind is that he opened the car door for me every time! Anytime we went anywhere, he'd get out of the car, run around to the other side and open the door for me! It was amazing. I never had anyone do that for me in my whole life. Like I say, I was a stripper. I was a stripper visiting from Canada."

Make that a stripper with a nasty temper—and a mean right hook.

Grammer and Csuhany's blissful courtship days came to an ugly end during the summer. On August 22, 1992, Sheriff's Deputies Kenton and Augarten responded to a frantic domestic call on Cornell Drive in Agoura, an arid community of ranch homes northwest of L.A. Kelsey had finally left his ramshackle rental in Van Nuys for the wide-open spaces of the Agoura area—but trouble still managed to find him.

When the deputies arrived at the house, they were surprised to be greeted by *Cheers'* Dr. Frasier Crane—although at that moment Kelsey Grammer looked nothing like the dapper TV psychiatrist. He was haggard and frazzled, and insisted the police do something about his girlfriend.

In their report, one of the deputies wrote:

"We responded to the location regarding a violently insane person. We contacted Grammer, Csuhany's live-in boyfriend, who said he and his girlfriend had been drinking and had gotten into a physical confrontation.

"Grammer said he and his girlfriend started arguing over a newspaper article written in the *Star* tabloid. Grammer said that the article gave a negative review on his relationship with Csuhany. They'd been arguing for several minutes when Csuhany walked up to him and punched him in the left eye. Grammer then walked out of the living room and into the bathroom, where he saw that his left eye was swelling and turning blue.

"We contacted Csuhany, who said that she and her boyfriend had been arguing over a newspaper article which was written about their relationship. Csuhany said that her boyfriend refused to discuss the newspaper article with her and started to walk out of the room. Csuhany said she was so upset when he refused to talk to her that she ran over and grabbed one of his arms with both of her hands.

"Csuhany said that her boyfriend refused to acknowledge her so she punched him in the face with her right fist. Her boyfriend did not strike her, but walked out of the room. We saw that Grammer had a bruised eye which was slightly swollen. Grammer refused any medical treatment. We did not see any visible signs of injury on Csuhany.

"Based on the statements made by Grammer and Csuhany, coupled with our observations, we arrested Csuhany for spousal assault. We offered Grammer an emergency protective order, which he declined."

They handcuffed Leigh-Ann and took her to the station, where the sheriff's deputies got to experience her wrath first-hand.

A supplementary report, also dated August 22, describes Csuhany's behavior once they got her to the station.

"The purpose of this report is to show a necessary use of force used upon Csuhany while she was in custody in booking cage #1 at the Lost Hills Station.

"At approximately 0815 hours I responded to the Lost Hills Station and contacted the acting watch commander, Sgt. R. Wallach, regarding the transportation of an injured female inmate—Csuhany—from Lost Hills Station to Sybil Brand Institute for Women jail," which is located in downtown Los Angeles, some thirty miles away.

"When I arrived at the Lost Hills Station, I saw that Csuhany was inside booking cage #1 and that she was banging on the metal screen with both hands. Csuhany was yelling and shouting obscenities in an obviously uncontrollable fit of rage. I then saw that Csuhany was bleeding from the middle finger of her right hand. As Csuhany would strike the metal screen with her hands, drops of blood from her injured hand were coming through the metal screen and landing on the metal counter in front of the booking cage.

"Due to Csuhany's self-inflicted injury coupled with her uncontrollable state, Sgt. Wallach, Deputy Izenman, Deputy Romanet, and I entered the booking cage in order to physically restrain her and prevent her from further injuring herself.

"As I attempted to restrain Csuhany by physically grabbing her right hand, Csuhany immediately jerked backward and became extremely combative. As I attempted to gain control of Csuhany's right arm, Sgt. Wallach grabbed her left arm, and together we physically pushed her downward onto the floor. While Csuhany was on the floor stomach down, she continued to resist and began kicking and screaming. Deputies Izenman and Romanet were able to gain control of Csuhany's legs. I managed to gain control of Csuhany's right arm as Sgt. Wallach gained control of her left arm. Sgt. Wallach and I had to physically place Csuhany's arms behind her back and were able to handcuff her.

"Although Csuhany was now handcuffed, she continued to kick and remained combative and uncooperative. It became necessary to place a hobble restraint on Csuhany's ankles to prevent her from kicking and possibly injuring her legs."

Cuffed and shackled like a felon, Leigh-Ann was driven to Sybil Brand, where her injured hand was tended to. A few days later, Detective Ed Young contacted Kelsey to talk about what had happened. Grammer calmly told Detective Young that he didn't want to talk about the case and suggested he speak with his attorney instead.

The next day, August 27, Grammer showed up at the Lost Hills sheriff's station and signed a "Victim's Request Not To Prosecute" form. Kelsey had to write down his reason for not wanting to pursue the matter.

"The incident was clearly unintentional, being motivated from the heat of an argument. Leigh-Ann and I are engaged and hoping to wed soon. I love her and have no desire to see anything proceed from what is a one-time occurrence! Thank you!"

Despite her own outrageous behavior, Grammer must have cringed when his fiancée told him detail after grisly detail of her experience while in custody. And all because of an argument over the *Star*. How he hated the tabloids! What could Kelsey ever do to make it up to her? Simply not filing charges wasn't enough—it was time to show her just how much he really loved her and just how sorry he was. As abruptly as their fight had begun, both Kelsey and Leigh-Ann swept the entire incident under the rug, and within days the fracas was just an unpleasant memory.

In reality, it was a preview of things to come.

It's strange that an actor so familiar with Shakespeare's work had no sense of foreboding. Instead of Kelsey stepping back and taking a long, hard look at his relationship with Leigh-Ann, he and Csuhany sneaked off and were married in a quickie ceremony in Nevada on September 11.

"We got married in Lovelock," Leigh-Ann says. "Lovelock is a tiny town about a hundred miles east of Reno. It was a secret mission because we wanted to get away from the press.

"When we decided to get married, we actually

planned two weddings. The first wedding was just to get married, and then we were going to have a second, formal wedding in Hollywood, with *People* magazine covering it. All the Hollywood bullshit.

"But we wanted to get married first, so we ran off and had a retired judge marry us in his home. We flew to Reno under aliases—Mr. and Mrs. Jones. After we landed, we rented a car and drove to Lovelock. We went to the courthouse, filled out the papers, and went to the judge's home. We didn't know the judge—Kelsey had been hooked up to the guy through his lawyer. It was a friend of a friend of a friend.

"While he performed the ceremony his wife sat behind us with a bowl of rice. Kelsey and I got married in their living room, wearing shorts.

"Pretty cheesy, huh?

"Actually, it was very nice. We didn't write our own vows—we were going to, but we figured we'd save that for the formal wedding."

Csuhany says one of the big reasons for marrying so abruptly was her residency status.

"We did it to get INS on the move. Kelsey was going to be leaving for Europe, and for me to go with him, I needed to have residency before I'd be able to leave the country and come right back in. When you're married, you have to file with immigration to get a temporary residency—but it can take six to eight months. If we had waited to get married and just done a big wedding, I wouldn't have been able to go to Europe with him because I wouldn't have my green card yet. So that was another reason we were married sooner than we originally planned."

Csuhany says that after the brief ceremony, she, Kelsey, and two friends who had acted as witnesses drove back to Reno.

"On our wedding night, I was in awe. Period. I couldn't believe I was married. Not only to him—I just couldn't believe I was married. Period.

"We went to our hotel and the people who were with us as witnesses were in the next room. Later, they made it sound [in the press] like I then said, 'Ha! Gotcha!' That as soon as we got married I said, 'Now that we're married I'm going to take you for everything you've got!'

The first thing I did say was, 'OK, you guys, get out of the room.' Not bitchy, not telling them to piss off—just that we want to be alone. Then Kelsey and I made love."

But there were reports that their newly wedded bliss might have had some rough edges.

According to some friends, Grammer and Csuhany showed up at a nearby Canoga Park pool hall the evening they returned from their brief Reno honeymoon.

"They came into the place the night after they got married and Leigh-Ann showed off her ring to everyone," says an employee. "It was pretty clear they hadn't gotten much sleep the night before—they looked awful. What was weird is that Kelsey was wearing a suit and Leigh-Ann had on a really nice dress.

It was reminiscent of his first marriage, to Doreen, that their vows were barely twenty-four hours-old and the lovebirds were already at each other's throats. The pool hall buddy says Kelsey was tired and told Leigh-Ann he wanted to go home, but she snapped right back at him that they'd leave when *she* said so.

Despite showing off her ring to their pool hall friends, Csuhany says the marriage was supposed to be a secret.

"We weren't going to tell anyone we were married—we'd just announce it at the reception of our second wedding. But it got to the point where it bothered me and it was hard to keep quiet about it. We were newlyweds and I was happy. It was hard to go, 'This is my boyfriend.' 'This is my girlfriend.' 'This is my fiancée.' I was Mrs. Grammer.

"We went to a charity event where Kelsey was speaking. He went up to the podium and did his deal, then he said, 'On a personal note, I'd like to introduce my new bride.'"

At least his sense of timing was still intact.

"Leigh-Ann can get really jealous and wants to make sure *nobody* else gets near Kelsey. Nobody female. She knows she's got a good catch. She also pretends he's never been married before. Part of it is that she's very young, and wants to believe that his wild days of womanizing and partying are over, and that she's the only one who matters in his life," a friend said.

"We're really, really in love," Leigh-Ann said at the time. "There's absolutely nothing that can come between us. We're trying to put the past behind us because we know our life together will be beautiful."

It seems amazing that Kelsey couldn't see that their individual wants, needs, and expectations were so vastly different. But friends agree that if nothing else, Kelsey was hot for Leigh-Ann—like

Fraiser was for Lilith—and chose not to think beyond their next physical encounter.

The news of Buckner's pregnancy broke in the media that October. Kelsey refused to talk about it, and thanks to his financial arrangement with Buckner, there was surprisingly little written about the circumstances surrounding Barrie's pregnancy. Kelsey saw that as a good sign, and felt as if he had won an important battle. In truth, he was really the big loser. Once again he had made his life that much more complicated—and that much less honorable.

Surely his grandfather would not approve of the course Kelsey's life was taking.

SEVEN

One striking thing about Grammer is that for all his sophisticated worldliness, for all his highbrow intellect, he seems to have a glaring tendency to engage in revisionist personal history, apparently hoping nobody else will notice. If it sounds smart enough and fluid enough, maybe the inconsistencies will be overlooked.

For example, even though published accounts of the 1990 sentencing report—in local L.A. papers, not the tabloids—prepared before his jail term revealed that Grammer began drinking at a young age and that he experimented with a variety of drugs, Kelsey would later deny he had ever indulged in such things. That it was just irresponsible press distortion.

If it weren't for other inconsistencies, maybe it would be easy to entertain the possibility that a couple of reputable publications had both erred. Except he did the same thing regarding the behavior that culminated with his being dragged off to jail. When talking later about the circumstances that led to his arrest, what to everyone present at the time had clearly been signs of a life out of control were now presented as little more than mischief.

"They certainly weren't capital crimes," Kelsey commented.

Perhaps it was a simple defense mechanism; perhaps he was trying to put an unsightly past behind him. Or maybe it was just his reaction to a growing resentment of the media in general. For example, when Csuhany's job as a stripper was uncovered, he expressed disdain for the reporters who dared reveal such a thing . . . even though it happened to be true. Csuhany also seemed to be of two minds about it all.

"I was in advertising," she told Tim Appelo, "but I got bored sitting in an office nine to five, so I became an exotic dancer. I guess dancing is advertising in a way. They make dancing sound a lot worse than it is. In Canada it's more of an art, but it is scummier down here."

And Csuhany should know, since she worked at a strip club in the United States during her early days with Kelsey. It's almost as if he knew, deep down, that he was embarking on the greatest folly of his life, and his instinct was to cover it up. If he was totally comfortable with it, there would be no real reason to run and hide. The truth was that this part of Csuhany's past was something Grammer just couldn't bring himself to acknowledge openly, whereas he did admit to living a large portion of his life in the fast lane.

"There will always be an element of a wild man

in me—but now I have a wild woman to share it with."

Little did he know how that sentiment would come back to haunt him.

When it became certain that Ted Danson was not going to return and that *Cheers* was really, finally ending, talk immediately began about developing a spin-off. While starring in a *Cheers* follow-up was no guarantee of success (think back to *Aftermash*), it was at the very least a shot at continuing stardom for whoever was chosen to wear the mantle.

At first it appeared that Woody Harrelson would get the nod from the *Cheers* producers and network executives. An early premise had Woody's addle-brained bartender character, Woody Boyd, buying the bar from Sam Malone; the hope was that the laughter would continue unabated in the place where everybody knows your name. There was only one hitch—Woody wasn't interested. His film career was poised to take off, and he had no interest in being tied down to a series again. And it was the right decision. Harrelson, who has gone on to star in films such as *Indecent Proposal* and *Natural-Born Killers,* is today a hot movie property.

So who, then?

John Ratzenberger and George Wendt, who played Cliff and Norm, respectively, were possibilities, but they apparently already had secured other development deals. Almost by process of elimination, it came down to Frasier, the character with the most layers. But that meant taking a chance on Kelsey, *Cheers'* problem child, who had drawn both exasperation and wrath from his employers.

The question then became, what spin-off?

Initially, says executive producer Peter Casey, he and *Frasier* cocreators David Lee and David Angell had considered a big-business format.

"One idea for a series with the *Frasier* format was that Kelsey would play a magnate modeled after Malcolm Forbes, running his empire from his bedroom after a motorcycle accident.

"Then the next idea was that *Frasier* would center around the life of the former *Cheers* psychiatrist as a radio personality, but the show seemed too similar to *WKRP in Cincinnati*."

Finally they hit on the winner. Frasier would be forced to reacquaint himself with his father.

"It was something many of us are going through right now," says David Lee. "Whenever you do a series, you're looking for an emotional hook. It gives depth and breadth to the characters."

Interestingly, Kelsey still almost didn't get the role. When they mapped out the concept for *Frasier*, John Lithgow was actually the show executives' first choice—but Lithgow passed. Against all probability, Kelsey was being handed an opportunity to star in his own series. But it wasn't without some sweaty palms. Even the men who hired Grammer still had doubts and fears.

"In the early stages of discussions, NBC asked pointedly, 'How's Kelsey been doing?'" admitted Casey. "And Jimmy Burrows said he was like a rock in the last two years of *Cheers*, in terms of being responsible and having his act together."

One has to wonder, compared to whom? Todd Bridges and Dana Plato of *Diff'rent Strokes*?

Little white lies aside, the former *Cheers* team—who also, not insignificantly, created another hit,

Wings—got their way. NBC president Warren Littlefield gave the go-ahead, even though he admitted he was well aware of Kelsey's past.

"I have been concerned and voiced my concern at times in Kelsey's life," Littlefield says. "But I had no hesitation when he said he was ready and wanted to do the show. I believed him."

Littlefield admitted later he was also a bit taken aback by the concept as pitched by the producers.

"They sat on the couch and said, 'We're presenting you *Frasier*, a family comedy.'

"'A *family* comedy?'

"'Don't worry,' they said. 'It's not about Mom and Dad and a couple of kids—but there *is* a living room.'"

Littlefield was willing to give them the go-ahead on whatever they wanted. Considering their track record, they deserved the chance to do the series the way they wished.

Kelsey's future was bright.

Unfortunately, the rose-tinted glasses he had worn when he married Leigh-Ann were about to shatter. Life with Leigh-Ann was increasingly difficult and stressful. The arguments came with furious regularity.

Csuhany readily accepts part of the blame.

"He's been a star for years, but here I am, from a small town in Canada. The money, the fame really bothered me at first. It always did for our entire relationship. I never really knew how to handle it, you know? At first it was kind of cool, people coming up and asking for autographs, wondering who I was.

"The first time it came out in *Star* magazine, we

were at a softball game and they put under the picture 'Kelsey Grammer would not say who is the red-haired cutie.' That was pretty cool. That was the first time I'd been around that scene, so at first it was cool—until the rags started coming out. Then I started hating it.

"It got to the point where I had to go to the grocery store at three o'clock in the morning. It got to the point where we could not go out to dinner— you literally could not wipe your ass—without somebody trying to take a picture. That really bothered me a lot.

"I didn't know how to handle it. Kelsey was always very nice to fans, but I'd be like, 'Look, we're trying to eat, so piss off!' Yeah, I said that once or twice. I tried to respect him, but I did say it. He said it comes with the territory. But he needed to be a little more understanding, because that was *his* territory for years—not mine."

Leigh-Ann had met Kelsey during the next-to-last season of *Cheers*, a time of maximum press exposure. For months Ted Danson had been the focus of an offscreen cliff-hanger: Would he re-sign for one last season or not? Danson was going through some messy personal problems of his own, having split from his wife of many years, Casey. Finally, after NBC nearly broke the bank to lure him back, Danson agreed to come back for a final season. Everyone was on board, and this set the stage for a high-profile final season—just what Leigh-Ann didn't need.

"We got married while they were on hiatus, so he came back to the show married—and here came the journalists digging into my past, coming out with brutal, brutal stories about Kelsey and me. Some true and some false."

And to be sure, their marriage *was* great fodder for both the supermarket tabloids and the TV tabloid-news shows. Both Grammer and Csuhany were indulging in heavy-duty substance abuse, and Leigh-Ann's jealousy and hair-trigger temper led to some ugly public spats.

"She was incredibly jealous," recalls one of Kelsey's friends. "If he even looked at another girl, she'd go wacko. One time I was with them when Leigh-Ann caught him looking at another girl. 'What are you looking at that slut for?' she said.

"Kelsey said he was just looking out the window, not at anybody. That's how it went—she was forever accusing him, and he was forever denying even window-shopping. It was really an explosive relationship."

In between the battling, though, there was still sexual heat pulsating between them. Once while on an airplane trip with the cast of *Cheers,* a coworker recalls Kelsey stepping out of the on-board bathroom with Leigh-Ann and announcing they had just joined the "mile-high club"—a phrase referring to people who have sex in planes while en route.

But when their passion subsided, the fights returned. There were scenes in Hollywood restaurants and in limos, but the worst scenes were at home—worse than any blaring tabloid headlines, worse than any of his friends expected.

"I wasn't the best wife—I admit it," Leigh-Ann says. "I just think that when you say for better or for worse, it means for better or for worse. But obviously it didn't mean that to him."

Csuhany tries to explain what happened, not only to their marriage but also to her personally.

"I didn't know how to deal with fame. Literally finding people hiding in bushes outside our doors, looking in windows, cameras and tripods found up in the hills behind our house—anywhere you went. It was ridiculous. It was tough. He knew how to deal with it, but it was very hard on me."

Csuhany says that for the most part, Kelsey kept a pretty level head about everything, even the fame—although he was human.

"Sometimes I'd see his head blow up," Csuhany recalls. "He would never say, 'I'm a star, I'm this and I'm that,' but it would pop out every once in a while. And when it did, I'd just look at him and say, 'OK, bud—you're no different than anybody else except you're on TV and have more money. That's all. You're a person like everyone else.' But overall, Kelsey was always really good to people."

The fame brought by *Cheers* resulted in considerable heartache for Leigh-Ann, but she also has fond memories of times on the set.

"I got along with all the cast on the show. It was a neat place, everyone was very close. Kelsey's best friends were crew guys, the grips. Plus he and Woody were tight friends. There were times Kelsey and I went out with Woody and his girlfriend, Laura, but there are very few real people in Hollywood. I hated that, and Kelsey didn't like it, either. He'd much rather go to the Red Onion or something and hang out at the bar with a bunch of real people.

"Fame." Csuhany spits the word out. "I can leave it. Stars get special treatment. These people are a million times worse than regular people—they're so high on themselves. I mean, I can't lie—I like the private jets, like the money, the travel.

"I have nothing against money, but the fame is brutal. Your life is an open book. You can't do anything without somebody knowing about it. It gets really tiring. We couldn't have a regular marital argument without somebody knowing about it."

But it wasn't just misconceptions by the press. Kelsey and Leigh-Ann seemed to be living parallel existences during their marriage, each interpreting a specific event in a vastly different way than the other. Their ability to communicate was on the verge of total collapse. Leigh-Ann gives an example of their mismatched visions.

"We had an argument on a plane one time, and later it came out in court papers that I had tried to fork him in the eye! In first class on the way to New York! I mean, let's get real! That's not true.

"What happened was, we got into the fight because he kept staring at this chick's ass—it was the stewardess—and it was really pissing me off. There's nothing wrong with taking a look or a glance, but I told him, 'If you stare any longer, your eyes will pop out of your head and stick to her ass!' We were eating dinner, so I had a fork in one hand and a knife in the other. I talk with my hands a lot. So I was talking with my hands and asked, 'Why do you have to do it?'

"And he said he wasn't doing it. Just like a man! They could be caught in bed with another woman and still say, 'It wasn't me!' So the court papers said I tried to stab him with a fork in first class on the way to New York. Yes, I was holding a fork, but I was eating dinner.

"Things just get built up and up."

On the other hand, friends of Grammer say he was at wits' end trying to put some semblance of civility into the marriage.

"Kelsey told stories about how out of the clear blue she would hit him, just smack him across the head or punch him in the gut just because she disagreed with something he said. He loved her so much, he let it go on.

"Another time they were out at dinner and Leigh-Ann started screaming at Kelsey, 'Where's the waiter?' Everyone in the place was staring, so Kelsey told her to calm down.

"And she started slapping him right there at the table. She also threw a plate at his head. He was screaming at her not to hurt his face, not to throw anything at his face."

But by all accounts, including Leigh-Ann's, Kelsey never so much as raised a hand to her.

"As bad as it got," Kelsey has said, "I would never dream of hitting her. In my book, anyone who strikes a woman is not a man."

The real beginning of the end started with wonderful news that should have brought them closer together than ever: Leigh-Ann was pregnant.

"We planned to have a baby," Csuhany insists. "That's why I was pregnant. I quit drinking, I quit partying, and we got the baby's room set up. During my whole pregnancy I had maybe two beers and a glass of wine; that's like half a glass at dinner or something, in total.

"That's good for someone like me, who parties like crazy. I was smoking harsh cigarettes before getting pregnant, but cut down to three or four extremely light Canadian cigarettes a day. That was hard, but I took the pregnancy seriously.

"See, I only had a one percent chance of getting pregnant, and he would always say, in front of friends and family, 'I'll get in there, I'll get in there, don't worry.'

"We planned to have a baby—we went to the doctor for the fertility stuff, the whole nine yards. We didn't do in-vitro but we did have appointments to do the fertility pills. *We planned this baby.* And then I found out I was pregnant.

"Obviously, because this was my first pregnancy, I was excited. But I don't know, I had a funny feeling because he just didn't seem happy about it. I expected him to be an excited father. But his mother was very happy."

Grammer seemed happy enough when he shared the news with the world, announcing the pregnancy on the *Arsenio Hall Show* in late April 1993. He added a curious aside, however, saying they didn't kiss the way they used to. But it seemed of little consequence considering that his career was going at full throttle. NBC was betting the bank on *Frasier*, and early reports indicated Kelsey had another winner on his hands. But the headiness he felt at work was tempered by difficulties at home.

Some of Kelsey's friends describe Leigh-Ann's behavior as nearly that of a crazed stalker. While Csuhany had by all indications cleaned up her act while pregnant, Kelsey continued to have guys' nights out, and it became a bone of contention.

"Leigh-Ann was certain Kelsey was out on the town with other women, leaving her pregnant at home alone," says one friend. "Several times when

Kelsey left the house for a night out, Leigh-Ann got in her car, chased him, and pulled him to the side of the road, screaming at him to come home."

Whatever joy he expressed to Arsenio Hall that night was fleeting. A few months later Leigh-Ann went on the warpath after reading a report in one of the supermarket tabloids that made her irate.

"When we went to Washington, D.C., Boston, and New York to promote his new show, we got into a big fight because a tabloid came out with an article saying Kelsey Grammer told a friend he'd always dreamed of having a bunch of different babies with a bunch of different women."

And considering that this child would have been his third, by three different women, the article may have contained more than a kernel of truth.

"Of course, my hormones were changing like crazy, and I got bitchy really quick. And I know not to believe this magazine, it's time to move on with my life, but it was tough. I'd only known Kelsey for a year ... it was tough getting used to, getting myself dragged through the papers every week," Leigh-Ann recalls, the painful memories squeezing words out of her mouth in a jumbled rush. "I flipped on him inside a hotel room. I lost it on him and started yelling and screaming."

The argument got out of control and propelled them into a session with a therapist. It was at that session that Kelsey revealed to Leigh-Ann that he wanted her to abort the baby.

"We had a meeting with the therapist and he's telling me he wants me to have an abortion. At the therapist's. It's a female therapist. I'm four months pregnant. I'm pro-choice and so is Kelsey, but I believe in [performing abortions during] the first six weeks. I don't believe in this whole shit after you get into your second trimester and you can feel the baby inside you!

"I was like, "Ahhhhhhh!' I lost it, and I left. I left the therapist's.

"I found out later he had the whole thing planned."

There was no turning back. Their relationship quickly spiraled out of control after the confrontation in the therapist's office, when Kelsey told his wife he didn't want the baby. Kelsey had had enough. Apparently the battle inside the Washington, D.C., hotel room had pushed him past the point of no return.

"He didn't come home that day. I called hospitals all night long. I called the police station all night long. I called every friend I could think of all night long.

"The next day, about four o'clock in the afternoon, I was with my girlfriend and all of a sudden there were eight cops and a private investigator knocking at my door. They handed me a stack of divorce papers about two inches thick that he had filed. Obviously he did all this behind my back. There was no way [he could have done all that] in twenty-four hours. He had a restraining order against me. He had an immediate evacuation order. I had ten minutes to pack one bag and get out.

"There's no way he could have done this in twenty-four hours," Leigh-Ann repeats. "He planned all this behind my back.

"Two nights before, we had made love and everything was OK. But it must have taken him at least two weeks to do this. There's no way from the time we went to our therapist, which was in the evening, until four o'clock the next afternoon, that he could have gotten all this shit.

"What judge would give a lifetime restraining order on something that I have no defense on? What he did is, his lawyers walked into court and said, 'My wife is trying to kill me . . . get a restraining order and immediate evacuation.' And the judge did it. It's a conspiracy. Obviously. Literally. How can a judge . . . without any kind of proof, police report . . . how?

"But he got it."

Csuhany still seems dumbstruck by the speed with which her marriage came crashing down around her.

"I was shocked. I lost it. I was so out of it I couldn't talk. I couldn't breathe. He wasn't there. I couldn't breathe. I fell down. I wandered around the house in shock, major shock. I was allowed to take my car and one bag. He had bought me a 1993 Mazda MX5 with twelve thousand dollars' worth of extras. Except I couldn't drive [because I was so upset].

"Later on I asked him why he bought me the car and he said he felt guilty he was leaving me."

It was the beginning of a particularly ugly chapter in Kelsey's life. On June 3, 1993, Allen Kelsey Grammer filed not only for divorce but also to have his marriage to Leigh-Ann annulled. He also charged Leigh-Ann with fraud and described her as being of "unsound mind."

Most interesting, Grammer also requested primary custody of "unborn baby Grammer due on December 7."

In a move out of character with the press-hating actor, Kelsey conducted an impromptu press conference outside his home, which he no longer shared with Csuhany.

"It's true there was in the past an element of the wild man in me. But she makes me look like a pussycat. It's something I hadn't reckoned with. The combination's not good, so we're getting divorced. There's no way we can save things now. It's sad, yes. But it's all been a terrible mistake."

Later he also said, "I am deeply pained. What otherwise should have been a happy time in my life has now turned sad and tragic."

Published reports at the time tell a very different story from Csuhany's regarding what led to the split. According to one article, a terrified Grammer showed up at a police station on June 2, begging for protection from his wife. He claimed she had threatened to shoot him and burn their house down.

The police took the complaint seriously because Leigh-Ann's own therapist—the same therapist Kelsey had seen with her—had called them earlier.

"Mr. Grammer had received a phone call from a therapist who treats his wife," said a policeman. "The therapist had also called the station, very upset. She said Mr. Grammer's wife had been seeing her for some time and that Leigh-Ann had a multiple-personality disorder. The therapist also said she was very violent.

"Leigh-Ann had told her she was going to burn down the house and kill Mr. Grammer. The therapist was sure the threats were real and broke a confidential relationship to keep Mr. Grammer from getting killed."

"Mr. Grammer also told us his wife had suicidal tendencies—and that he'd been the victim of spousal abuse for some time. He was very tense and he was trembling."

But because no physical confrontation had actually occurred, all the police could do was advise Kelsey to stay away from home and ask the court to issue a restraining order. Which he did—in addition to making sure he was surrounded by personal protection.

"Her fears of Kelsey cheating on her turned to threats—and fantasies of killing him," said a friend. "Her threats against Kelsey have him so terrified and he's so paranoid that he's hired bodyguards. And he's so convinced she's crazy, he's asking for custody of the baby."

The divorce was bound to bring another embarrassing round of publicity for Grammer—but better now than after *Frasier* was on the air. However callous that may sound, it was obviously one of the factors that led him to leave Csuhany. Grammer says as much himself.

"Part of my decision to resolve my situation by divorcing Leigh-Ann was out of respect for the upcoming obligation of *Frasier*," Kelsey says. "I knew I would not be able to do well if my personal life were still in that position.

"When I look at it now, it was just a smart move."

For Leigh-Ann, it simply brought a sense of doom.

"Three days later," she says, referring to being ordered out of the house, "I went to the Malibu Inn, just to spend some time by myself. I got some blow, got some wine, some pills, and I tried to kill myself. I took sixty Tylenol.

"I called my therapist. She called 911. I guess when they found me I was dead. Anyway, I was in ICU for two days. They didn't know whether I was going to live or die.

"Kelsey did not come to the hospital. He did not call or send flowers. I was told that many people called him and said, 'We don't know if your wife is going to live or not.' And he still never came.

"When I came out of it, we did tests to see if the baby was still OK—and it was. The baby was healthy, no problem. That's on a medical report. But I was told by my therapist that if I had an abortion Kelsey would come back to me. I didn't want to. I was pressured by the doctors, and the hospital pressured me.

"'If you have an abortion Kelsey will come back.' That's all I kept hearing, so I agreed to it on the condition that he be there when I went in. I was told he agreed to it.

"I was told he was on the way to the hospital. They drugged me, brought me down, and they asked me if I wanted to do this. All I remember is crying and saying, 'No, no, no. Where's Kelsey? Where's Kelsey?'

"He didn't come to the hospital. He didn't show up. He didn't send a flower. He didn't call. He didn't do nothing. Obviously he wanted me to have an abortion so he wouldn't have to pay thousands a month in child support. So then I got out of the hospital and went to my sister's for a couple of months."

What Grammer did do was release a statement.

"I am deeply saddened by the events leading to the aborted pregnancy. Although annulment proceedings are under way, I had dreamed of raising the baby in a stable and loving environment."

But the initial June filing was only the beginning of a bitterly contested divorce, with each side filing charges and countercharges. It was sensational in the truest sense of the word.

On August 9, the court awarded Leigh-Ann temporary support from Kelsey, to the tune of $7,500 a week, which no doubt struck his "every woman is out to get my money" nerve. Grammer shot back ten days later with both barrels blazing.

In papers filed August 19, less than a month before *Frasier*'s September 16 debut, Grammer outlined in stark legalese why he was asking for the marriage to be annulled: intentional misrepresentation, false promise, fraudulent concealment, negligent misrepresentation, assault and battery, and intentional infliction of emotional distress.

Grammer told the court that Leigh-Ann had lied when she told him she wanted to marry him solely out of love and for no other reason. He claimed her ulterior motives were becoming a legal permanent resident and financial gain. He also charged that Leigh-Ann had deceived him into going ahead with the marriage.

"In justifiable reliance on said misrepresentation of defendant, plaintiff [Grammer] married defendant months earlier than he planned, in a ceremony conducted on or about 9/11/92," reads the filing.

"In further justifiable reliance on said misrepresentations, plaintiff spent substantial sums for defendant's benefit and support, including ... clothing, travel, automobiles and insurance.

"In committing aforesaid acts against plaintiff, defendant acted fraudulently and with malice and oppression and intended to oppress and cause injury to plaintiff.

"Plaintiff is therefore entitled to an award of punitive damages against defendant."

Grammer was only warming up.

"Defendant promised to sign a prenuptial agreement ... prior to 9/11/92 which would provide that all earnings during the contemplated marriage ... would remain plaintiff's separate property, including all earnings from plaintiff's work on the television show *Cheers*.

"Defendant promised to continue attending individual and joint therapy sessions for an indefinite period of time but not less than three months after parties were married.

"At the time defendant made said promises ... she had no intention of performing them. The promises were made ... with the intent to induce plaintiff to go ahead with and expedite plans to marry ... and to spend plaintiff's money for the support and benefit of the defendant."

Financial matters aside, the most startling disclosures were allegations about Csuhany's mental health—or lack thereof.

"In 1992, prior to September 11, defendant failed to disclose that she had a serious psychological disorder known as borderline personality disorder and further failed to disclose to plaintiff that she had been hospitalized and/or under care and treatment for this condition and that this condition left defendant with an unstable and vindictive personality."

Next came what was, even in lawyer-speak, a harrowing account of violence Grammer said he suffered at the hands of Leigh-Ann.

"On various occasions within the preceding one year, defendant repeatedly assaulted and battered plaintiff by violently slapping plaintiff in the face, pulling plaintiff's hair, scratching and biting plaintiff, kicking plaintiff, discharging firearms at plaintiff, holding a knife to plaintiff's throat in a threatening manner and threatening to cut him, holding a fork near plaintiff's eye and threatening to stab him, and throwing various objects at plaintiff with the intent to commit great bodily harm.

". . . Plaintiff was placed in great fear for his safety and physical well-being."

The papers indicate that Grammer was in such desperate straits that he sought help from therapy. But the abuse wore on.

"In addition to the foregoing conduct, defendant on various occasions within the preceding one year shouted at plaintiff in public in a rude, insolent, and violent manner and used loud profanity and vulgarity and threatened plaintiff with death and bodily harm. In addition . . . defendant threatened plaintiff that if he ever left her, she would ruin him by making false and demeaning statements about plaintiff to the press."

Hoping to temper the publicity this virulent divorce would generate, Grammer succeed in convincing the judge to seal the divorce papers—an increasingly common occurrence even though sealings are supposed to be ordered only when there are extenuating circumstances, usually when children or molestation charges are involved. But more and more press-shy celebrities are being allowed to conduct what are supposed to be public court procedures in private.

In this case, however, sealing the divorce papers did little, if anything, to stem the tide of publicity.

EIGHT

Obviously it was much more than just the pressures of fame that came between Kelsey Grammer and Leigh-Ann Csuhany and precipitated the destruction of their marriage with so much white heat. But who can ever pinpoint the exact moment when things take a fatal turn?

There was anger and resentment on both sides, and little events took on significant proportions.

"I felt he did things behind my back," says Leigh-Ann. "There are things I found out later on. He paid Cerlette's rent for six months behind my back. We were together for six months before I found out. He was still letting her charge stuff on his charge card.

"I said, 'What do you do—hang on to every squeeze you've ever had in your life?'

"He said, 'Oh, no—she could take me to court because we were common-law.' He said they were together for seven years. It pissed me off. He'd do stuff like that behind my back.

"And I was with him twenty-four hours a day, which is another thing that fucked us up."

Grammer made it clear by his stream of court filings that it was really, truly over. Leigh-Ann greeted the newly filed divorce papers by trying to hold her head up high and, it seems, trying not to dodge her part in the devastation. While she denied most of the claims of overt physical violence, she did admit she had attended spousal-abuse counseling.

"It was mainly verbal abuse," Csuhany explains. "I hit him *once*, a week before we got married, which is well documented. I won't discuss it. I went to jail that night. And I was out twelve hours later on a Sunday on twenty-five thousand dollars bail. Never heard about it again.

"I was jealous when we were married," Leigh-Ann confesses. "I was insecure a lot. I'm not going to deny that. It bothered me a lot when women threw panties at my husband. I didn't know how to handle it properly. I knew in the back of my mind, but it was hard to control my feelings.

"Like I admitted before, I went to a therapist; they suggested I go on Prozac. My temper was short. I agreed to it. When I got pregnant I had to go off all my meds. Anyone who has been on Prozac can tell you, you get addicted to it. When it's taken away from you that quickly, it makes you irritable. It is nothing mental. It is a chemical thing.

"Not only that, but anyone who has been pregnant knows what a pregnant woman is like! Your hormones are going a hundred miles an hour, you have mood swings. So I'd get a little more erratic when I was pregnant—and he left me for that."

Csuhany recounts her irritability and lack of patience.

"He'd come in and I would tell him to leave me alone. 'Don't touch me.' But it wasn't all the time.

"He told me the last straw was when I ripped the phone out of the wall in Washington, D.C., when we were fighting over that article. When I read that article I got mad and ripped the phone out of the wall, which is not bad. I mean, I didn't pick up a gun and blow his head off, which they're trying to make it sound like I did.

"I'm not going to deny I wasn't an angel while we were married. I'm not the easiest girl to get along with. But there was one thing: I was married to him and I loved him to death. And when I said for better or for worse, when I said for richer or for poorer, I meant for richer or for poorer, and I meant till death do us part.

"And obviously those words to him don't mean shit. He could have done other things instead of dropping the bomb the way he did. He could have just left me. He could have had a separation for six months. I would have dealt with that, to get things clear."

But Grammer apparently made an all-or-nothing decision, believing his tumultuous personal life could threaten his career in general, and *Frasier* specifically. Knowing NBC had backed him—at a salary reported to be in the range of $200,000 an episode—and the series with a considerable chunk of money, he decided there was no turning back in his marriage. It was time to move on and let the dust settle.

Although he maintains he was primarily a victim

in the marriage, he accepts that his choice of women hasn't always been the wisest. And he philosophizes as to why.

"I always was attracted to people who didn't have boundaries," he admits. "People who would just do anything, anywhere, and I'd sort of go, 'Oops.' That's where it starts, but it can get worse than that. You can be spit on by your wife in front of the President of the United States—that's a good one.

"I really can't say much more than that because there's a gag order on it. But my definition of bad is very loose. Human experience is basically good. I've always tried to stick with the golden mean— nothing in excess, everything in moderation."

Obviously the road to L.A. County Jail was paved with good intentions.

"I have, by a series of excesses, found moderation," Grammer counters. "But never to my shame or regret, really. People would interpret some of the things that have happened to me as being shameful, but I don't. I see them as watermarks on the way to becoming a higher-evolved human being. I'm the whole ball of wax.

"At some level, you are the sum total of your experience—and my experience has been pretty interesting. I wouldn't trade it for the world."

If Kelsey has had one sticking point on the road of evolution, it does appear to have been the women in his life. His utter silence regarding his mother is deafening—it's as if she doesn't exist in his frame of reference. Tales of his bitterness at ex-spouses and girlfriends to whom he is financially obligated are a recurring theme: an undisclosed sum to Barrie Buckner for child support of daughter Greer, the settlement with Leigh-Ann, money paid out to Cerlette after leaving her, even the $7,000 a month to Doreen to help rear his elder daughter, eleven-year-old Spencer. Doreen, who at one point claimed in divorce papers she was forced to waitress until two o'clock in the morning to help support Spencer, remains a particularly distasteful subject.

"He cannot stand writing the monthly checks to her," Leigh-Ann says. "I've seen him many times. He literally twitches, has this horrible look of disgust on his face when he has to go in and sign the checks. He probably does the same thing with me," she chuckles.

"Now he has three of them he has to do every month."

And yet this is the same man who regularly volunteers his time and money to charity, and is generous with fans as well.

"He does a *lot* of charity," Csuhany confirms. "He rarely turned down any kind of TV shot when I was with him. He was always good to his fans. I've met a lot of stars who are total assholes to their fans. He was not."

It's as if he initially gives of himself out of genuine generosity, but once he feels he's even slightly taken for granted, he sees it as proof that he was being played for a chump all along. Even if the claim, like Doreen's, is one that is legally entitled to be made, he acts as if it is proof of personal betrayal.

Csuhany says she's stopped trying to figure it out. "Deep down, Kelsey is an unhappy person.

Money and fame help, but he gets down a lot. Who knows what goes on in his mind? I'll tell you what was the worst thing that ever happened to Kelsey and still rips him apart to this day—his sister. That was probably *the* major tragedy in his life. As far as his father and half-brothers go, I don't think so. He hardly knew them. I mean, yes, it's sad that his father was murdered, but he barely knew him.

"[What happened to] his sister was definitely the killer. He talked about it all the time. He cried when he talked about his sister. I held him and said I was sorry, but it was very tough."

The most important person in his world, the person he was closest to, left Kelsey—forever. It's understandable that he would fear suffering that kind of loss again, even if the death is symbolic, as when a relationship sours or a marriage goes terribly wrong. If he tests people enough, or sets the standards high enough, or picks people who will never meet his standards, he'll create circumstances that will successfully prevent any possibility of getting too close to someone and limit their ability to cause him pain when the relationship inevitably fails.

The unbelievable soap opera that was his marriage to Leigh-Ann was sobering for Kelsey and further raised his defenses. He wondered aloud if there was a woman alive who could put up with him. "I'm no angel," he said. "I doubt I'll ever marry again because I require too long a leash. Marriage made me feel tied to a ball and chain."

However, Grammer says he absolutely believes in monogamy during marriage.

"That was never the problem. Women flirt and

act feminine when it comes to snaring their husbands. But barely is the ink on the marriage certificate dry and they're trying to dominate their man."

Not surprisingly, Kelsey's women had a slightly different take on his attitude.

Cerlette agreed with one thing, though. "No leash is long enough for Kelsey. I don't know what he saw in Leigh-Ann, but she was lucky to marry him. He's a warm and wonderful man, a beautiful man. I loved him with a passion. I still love him and I know he loves me—but the guy's a bachelor through and through.

"He's kind and loving but he's also so self-destructive. Sometimes I think he feels he doesn't deserve what he has in life."

Or simply feels guilty that he's still alive.

Csuhany is more blunt. "It can't be everyone else's fault all the time. He's self-destructive but blames everyone else. He blames Leigh-Ann, Cerlette—not Kelsey. There's a pattern here. But it can't possibly be everybody else's fault all the time."

Reflection on his relationships with women and his vulnerable psyche would have to wait. The show was about to go on. With crossed fingers and bated breath, Kelsey and NBC launched *Frasier* on September 16, 1993. Neither needed to have worried—it was an instant hit.

Suddenly Kelsey's future was as bright as ever. So was his bank account. As he climbed the next rung of stardom he not only achieved the riches and adulation every TV actor dreams of, but he basked in critical praise as well. *Frasier* was every bit the quality show *Cheers* had been—and it was everything NBC had hoped for and more.

His success eased the pain of his ongoing divorce battles and of the lengthy process of breaking away from Leigh-Ann as a presence in his life. But it was hard. Especially when Csuhany continued to let the world know how much she still loved him.

"I'd trade anything to get him back. I'm still hanging on to the hair of hope."

A snowball had a better chance in hell. Kelsey would not ever come back. He had hit the ground running and wasn't about to slow down.

The last time Csuhany and Grammer spoke was about a month after they split up. Leigh-Ann found out his new phone number, which had been changed since she left, by using a secret system they had developed when together. They had a code of repeating numbers, so she began dialing randomly, hoping to find him.

"And I actually got him. He answered the phone, and all I said was, 'I love you.' And all he said was, 'I love you, too,' and he hung up. I was hopeful he'd come around. I saw a psychiatrist twice a week. I went to spousal counseling once a week. I did everything I could to try and make it better. He never tried. He never had any intention of coming back."

Csuhany had finally gotten the point.

The divorce was granted in December 1993, with terms of the settlement under seal and both parties agreeing not to disclose them. But the acrimony still clouded the air.

"Her rides in the limousine are over," announced Grammer's attorney, Leon Bennett. "We pray she is sent back to where she belongs . . . which is as far away as possible."

In fact, there was speculation that someone in Grammer's camp had called the U.S. Immigration and Naturalization Service in hopes of having Csuhany deported—or at least to intimidate her into going away quietly. But if Kelsey thought he'd heard the last of Leigh-Ann, he was sadly mistaken.

In a move that seemed overtly designed to get under his skin, Csuhany went back to stripping, billing herself as the "wife of the *Cheers* star." It worked. Grammer wanted to tear his thinning hair out.

"She's out to cause me maximum embarrassment, to make me a laughingstock," Kelsey remarked about his estranged wife's career move. "I regret the day I ever set eyes on her. Can you believe she's told me she'll have my name in lights outside every strip joint in the country?

"I'll never shake that woman. She had nothing when we met, now she has a hundred grand in the bank—and she's still not satisfied. What in God's name does she want?"

Csuhany was nonplussed by Grammer's tirade.

"I was an exotic dancer when we met, so it's hypocrisy for him to have even the slightest objection. Kelsey's a very sweet man and I love him, but he can't believe his luck, he got off so lightly. He begged me to give up my job when we met and I did. Now that it's over, I have to fend for myself."

And as a bright light on the celebrity stripper circuit, Csuhany could command up to a thousand dollars a night—not bad for a girl from a small town in Canada. Besides, she says she needs to stash money away because who knows how long it will be before her life can get back to normal.

"It's really hard to move on when you're constantly reminded—any book, any magazine you pick up just standing in line at the grocery store. And people recognize you, especially just standing in line at the grocery store. It's really difficult when you see people staring at you and hear them whisper, 'That's the crazy wife.' Especially when meeting men.

"I meet a guy I really like and I try to move on with my life, then they find out who I am and get scared away! Literally."

Csuhany says her reputation, courtesy of the tabloids, makes it tough to get a romance going.

"Haven't you seen all the crap?" She dramatically announces mock headlines. "'Threatens to Kill Him with a Gun!' 'Tries to Cut His Penis Off!' My God. Or my favorite, 'Puts Ben-Gay in His Underwear!'

"That's not true, but when I read it I laughed my ass off. I should have thought of that—except Kelsey doesn't even own a pair of underwear. Never has. The last time he wore underwear was when they made him for a TV commercial."

Their lives were going in opposite directions, and Grammer was determined to keep his momentum. He was tireless in his promotion of the show, appearing on talk shows everywhere and setting up interviews one after another. He covered every aspect of the groundwork necessary to launch his show.

And in doing so, he made a conscious decision to bare his soul. He was through trying to fight the media. As the line from *Apocalypse Now* says, rather than fear the horror, he was going to make it his friend. Or maybe it was the result of the therapy he was in. Either way, a new Kelsey was emerging phoenixlike from the ashes.

"I am in therapy," Kelsey acknowledges. "There's no question I need it. Oh, yeah—about twice a week. And I'm really happy about it. It's a great help."

His weekly talk sessions are helping teach Kelsey to relax and handle the obstacles as they come and not to hide from the truth, even if it's going to appear in print.

"Celebrity has its perils, though they are not insurmountable. Your private life is sort of a casualty, but it comes with the territory. Oh, you didn't think this might happen when you decide to become a star? If your dream didn't include bad parts, you were just being an idiot.

"A long time ago I sat down and thought, why are they picking on me? Then I thought, Well, I'm on television. Who else are they going to write about?

"Everybody believes we are the luckiest people in the world. And in some ways we are. We're the people they love—and love to hate. They love it when we make a mistake and prove we're not perfect. There's a sort of vengeful glee in it."

Kelsey shrugs.

"Anyway, I thought there's nothing to really hide because everybody's going to write about it anyway. My viewpoint is if it comes from my mouth, that will get people to stop talking about it. So I've talked about things and I really have no apologies to make.

"I've certainly made some mistakes, but I'm not sorry for the things that have happened to me or the things I have mistakenly done. The best thing about life, in my opinion, is that you can grow, you can fix things, you can make amends, if you will, for things that people may think you may need to."

As an example, Grammer brings up his well-documented drug problem, arrests, and jail term—occurrences he calls landmark events.

"Yeah, there's been a lot of stuff. I was irresponsible about fulfilling my obligations to the courts—that's the way I've been about a lot of things. And I paid for it," he says, referring to jail and his community-service punishment.

"Picking up trash is no less dignified than anything else. What *was* humiliating was realizing I had to do something about my drug problem. I got into trouble with drugs. I knew I was overdoing it but I said to myself, 'I won't do this too long.' I don't recommend them, but I'll never deny I had a ball."

Most amazing to everyone on *Frasier* is the turnaround Kelsey made in insulating his work against the outrageous fortunes of his private life.

John Mahoney, who plays Grammer's retired cop dad, marvels at Kelsey's professionalism. "He's never late. I've never, ever seen him lose his temper. He's very open about the whole thing. There's not a shred of tension. Whatever's gone on in his personal life has never affected the quality of his work.

"He's unfailingly good-hearted and good-spirited on the show. His concern while we're working is with the script and what we're working on."

Grammer is fiercely protective of his new series and his castmates. Whereas many an actor might feel threatened being surrounded with the high-wattage talent John Mahoney and David Hyde Pierce bring to the show, Grammer revels in it.

"That's what's good. I never in my life want to back away from someone who's gifted and talented. You *want* to surround yourself with the best possible group of people in the world and just throw yourself into it.

"In terms of my career, this is the height. This is something I was hoping to achieve. I got my own show and it's a good show. I'm proud of it. All the stuff that happened to me before," he says, meaning the string of personal crises, "that was basically, I think, in preparation to get to the point of having this much responsibility.

"Also, my life has been full of a lot of richness and joy. I love life—I think possibly because of the tragedies that have been marked along the way."

The concept of family, whether good or bad, never seems to be very far away from the surface of Kelsey's thoughts. It's ironic that in *Frasier*, his character is coming to terms with the family he has.

"What's a nice parallel for me is that I'm discovering a family I never had. Kelsey gets to come along for the ride. I have a relationship with a father and a brother—I never had any of those things. So it's fascinating to talk to 'my dad.' It's been interesting for a man to explore the relationships between the men in his life."

As for his relationship with Frasier, Kelsey says the two of them share certain traits, not the least of which is a wild streak simmering just below the surface, an emotional Mount St. Helens that, if left unattended, could blow at any moment.

"We've grown together," he says of himself and his character. "I'm a bit more haphazard and a bit more casual. But there's a side of me that would rather sit around listening to classical music at night and reading a good book than to be hanging out with a bunch of contemporaries going crazy—even though I tend to do the other thing."

Frasier's success also afforded Kelsey a certain amount of largesse. In one of the series' highest-rated shows, Bebe Neuwirth returned for a one-shot appearance as Dr. Crane's ex-wife, who flies in to see him in Seattle, where the show is set.

Although he and Neuwirth are hardly buddies, Grammer says he still does see some of the old gang.

"I see Ted," Kelsey said of *Cheers* star Danson, who would also appear as a guest star during the 1995 February sweeps. "I see Woody, and I saw George Wendt yesterday. We get along fine, but we didn't hang out together. The women I don't see as much. I do speak with Kirstie, but Shelley left so long ago. . . ."

Now that the tables have turned, Grammer is playfully snide when it comes to his old nemesis. He recalls the time he mentioned during an interview that the question he was most frequently asked during his time in jail was, how is it to work with Shelley Long? When asked why he thought the general prison population had been so enchanted with Ms. Long, Kelsey pondered with optimum dramatic flair.

"How can I say this diplomatically? . . . Shelley,

to many people, is very attractive. I, um, never thought of her that way. I just thought of her as someone I worked with, so I couldn't offer any insight into Shelley's charms.

"But frankly, the inmates asked about everybody. What's Woody like? Well, he's a nice guy. What's George like? Great guy. Does he really drink beer? Well, not on the show, but George does like beer.

"It was the normal questioning drill that you go through during a two-minute conversation."

However, Kelsey was much more pointed about his onetime *Cheers* castmate the week that *Frasier* hit the top ten—and Shelley's ill-fated series *Good Advice* slid to the bottom ten.

"Kelsey gathered everyone together on the set and offered a toast to Shelley and the continued success of her show," says a friend. "It was really an ironic turn of events, considering what hell she caused him when he first joined *Cheers*. It had to be just a delicious moment for Kelsey."

And to think Grammer was at first wary of continuing with the Frasier Crane character. "I thought originally that Frasier should die with *Cheers*," Grammer admits. "But I like him. He tries to stay true to his word. He's a decent chap who's overwhelmed at times, but he's still staggering on with rejoicing. Frasier is lovable because he's quite comfortable being flawed. He realizes that even though he's got all these pretensions, he's sincerely trying to do the best he can from day to day. He's lovable because he's so human.

"Things never go the way he really wants them to, but he's got a good heart, he gets on with his life. He's the classic of what I hope to do in life. He staggers onward, rejoicing—somehow."

At times it does seem as if Grammer is talking much more about himself than the character he plays on television.

"There's a part of me I lend to Frasier. I certainly have a broader base than he does, but I was aware of that part of me a long time ago. Now he's like an alter ego that I get to play with. He gets to come out."

But for his part, Kelsey tried to stay in more—and thereby stay out of trouble. But it wasn't always easy. He had a lifetime of bad habits that were hard to break. Despite his resolve to walk the straight and narrow, Kelsey occasionally slipped off the path, muddying his shoes.

And sometimes nearly drowning in a ditch.

In November 1993 yet another potentially career-ending scandal snaked into his life, bringing with it the most serious allegations Kelsey had ever faced. This wasn't the self-inflicted crime of drinking or drugs—this was rape.

It began at a reunion of old friends.

In July 1993, a month after slapping divorce papers on Leigh-Ann, Kelsey traveled to the Somerset Hills Hotel in Watchung, New Jersey. He was happy to find any excuse to leave California, and this time he went back East to visit with some longtime friends, including the father and stepmother of a teenager named Jane[1]. Grammer brought along his daughter Spencer for the visit.

According to later reports, when all of the adults

---

[1]Her name has been changed to protect her identity.

went out later on the night of July 7, 1993, Jane stayed at the hotel to baby-sit Spencer. She also spent the night in Grammer's suite, ostensibly so Kelsey could attend a business meeting the next day. It was that night that Kelsey's alleged first sexual encounter with Jane took place.

The second was in Arizona.

Later that same summer, in August, Kelsey suggested to Jane's stepmother that they all take a trip to the Enchantment Resort in Sedona, Arizona. Spencer would go along, too. Kelsey no doubt explained that he could use some time in the desert to regroup after the grueling legal battles he and Leigh-Ann were waging. Grammer even offered to pay for the trip, and made the reservations for August 27 to 29. Three rooms were reserved. The stepmom was pleasantly surprised and later commented why.

"This was the first time in the thirteen years that I'd known Kelsey that he had been so generous toward me."

It was there that authorities would later contend another sexual encounter took place.

No one disputes the fact that Jane baby-sat for Spencer that night in July. And no one disputes the fact that Jane and Kelsey began *some* type of relationship that night—a relationship that led to many phone calls and other in-person visits. But that is where the agreement ends.

In the months following that all-important July evening, Jane's parents became suspicious about her contact and association with Kelsey, a man twenty-two years her senior. When the girl's stepmother called a friend who worked for Kelsey, she was shocked when the friend, Rudy Hornish, gave her a piece of startling advice: "Watch out for your daughter."

Hornish said he had seen letters written by Jane to Kelsey and that the letters strongly hinted they shared some sort of sexual relationship. The parents began to investigate, and their suspicions led them to a shocking discovery—Kelsey regularly left messages for Jane on a phone service called Teen Line.

They felt their worst fears had been confirmed and believed the messages were not only sexually inappropriate, but proof that Kelsey had seduced Jane. They immediately called their lawyer, John Esposito, a Harvard Law School graduate working out of Brooklyn, New York.

Then they called the police.

Armed with what they had uncovered, they confronted Jane, who steadfastly refused to admit that anything wrong had taken place.

In September of 1993, Jane's parents discovered the taped messages she had been receiving from Kelsey. Undaunted, she continued to deny that anything untoward had happened between her and Kelsey. Unsure what to do next, her parents put her into therapy. But somewhere around this time the girl, who says she *was* in love with Kelsey—and believed the feeling was mutual—tipped the actor off that her parents were aware of their relationship.

To say it was the last thing Kelsey needed would be an understatement. Grammer was just emerging from the nightmare that had been his second marriage and was unquestionably vulnerable and emotionally fragile. Plus he was under pressure to carry the weight of *Frasier*, a new series faced with high expectations. Anything less than a hit would have been seen as a failure. Now he was potentially facing a big-time jail term if he should somehow be convicted of this.

Although he never so much as acknowledged that yet another scandal was brewing in his life, the affair was indeed taking on a life of its own, though it was still completely out of the public eye. Very few people knew what treacherous waters Kelsey was wading in. It is probably one reason he threw himself into *Frasier* so totally—it helped keep his mind off what he knew could abruptly kill the show, not to mention his career.

The news went national in November. The *National Enquirer* and television's *A Current Affair* trumpeted the allegations that Kelsey had been sexually involved with a fifteen-year-old girl who had baby-sat for his daughter Spencer. This raised eyebrows even among the most jaded of Hollywood observers.

The allegations hung in the air like a cloud of poison gas. After the story broke, Grammer immediately released a statement denying all charges—the same day Jane gave a statement to the prosecutor's office in Somerset County, New Jersey. The girl, who lived in Phoenix, quickly went into hiding as the media descended on her and her family.

New Jersey prosecutor Nicholas Bissell had reopened the investigation his office had earlier closed because of the girl's refusal to cooperate.

Now all Grammer could do was wait for the

other shoe to drop. He was forced to live in a strange sort of suspended animation while the investigation slowly wound its way from New Jersey to Arizona and back again. At times it was so out of sight that it was almost possible to forget it hadn't all been just another bad dream.

Using a credo from Alcoholics Anonymous, Kelsey tried not to worry about something over which he had no control. He forced himself to look forward. And there were plenty of good things to see.

By February of 1994 *Frasier* had established itself as a solid hit and Kelsey was as sought-after a personality as there was in Hollywood. All the talk shows wanted him, and he was coveted as a host too. Gladly willing to promote *Frasier* any chance he got, Grammer agreed to cohost the Soap Opera Digest Awards along with *Days of Our Lives* sexpot Lisa Rinna, who also happened to be Harry Hamlin's main squeeze. The rationale was that Grammer had once been on *Another World,* even if it was just as a day player.

The awards show was produced by none other than the Hollywood icon Dick Clark, who has made a career of his conservative appearance and straight-arrow lifestyle. For Kelsey to host the show was like *Father Knows Best* meeting Al Bundy.

The awards ceremony was held at the venerable Beverly Hilton Hotel, owned by Merv Griffin. Grammer found himself amid Hollywood heavyweights. Despite all that had happened, he was still being accepted as part of the mainstream, at least on the surface. He was positively giddy during rehearsal and quickly put everyone at ease.

Both Grammer and Rinna were given complimentary suites at the hotel, and after rehearsal they retired to their rooms. Except Kelsey was very late in coming out of his.

"As it's getting closer and closer to air time, people were beginning to wonder where exactly Kelsey was," says a member of the production. "Everyone wondered if he was all right.

"The show was being broadcast live back East, so it wasn't as if there was any leeway when it came to starting the show. Finally, a couple of people from *Soap Opera Digest*, the magazine that sponsors the awards, went up to Kelsey's suite to make sure he wasn't sick or something."

Grammer was fine—in fact, he was feeling no pain.

"There he was, sitting on the sofa, guzzling white wine. The magazine people were in a state of shock. They saw their careers passing before their eyes, while Kelsey just sat there with a delightful smile on his face."

Now it was a game of beat the clock. With the seconds ticking by, the audience in its place in the Grand Ballroom, and the cameras about to go live, Grammer was hustled into a cold shower. They barely took the time to dry him off before literally dressing him in his tux. As they were still buttoning his pants he was already being escorted downstairs to the ballroom.

"They got him backstage in the nick of time," says the eyewitness. "After that, all they could do was pray he'd pull it off. At the beginning of the show, you could see that his hair was still wet— they hadn't had time to blow-dry it.

"Fortunately Kelsey's a pretty funny drunk, and miraculously nobody in the audience seemed to notice he was tipsy. It was hardly a stellar performance, but the Soap Opera Digest Awards are hardly the Oscars, either, so it turned out OK.

"But it wasn't an experience the awards people are likely to want to repeat."

Not only was Kelsey propelled into therapy by his marriage and divorce, but he had also made an effort to attend AA meetings more regularly, although he slipped often. About a week after the awards show, Kelsey turned up at one of his regular meetings and got up to speak before the assembled group.

"He admitted that he slipped," says a friend who was present. "Kelsey showed a lot of remorse and needed to talk it over with everyone. He said he had tried to pinpoint what made him slip and had come to a couple of conclusions.

"The first was that even though his show was a big hit, he still harbored a secret fear inside that somehow he'll find a way to lose it all. He said there's a certain pressure in *staying* successful that's different from the anxiety of *wanting* to be successful.

"And he's still having trouble getting past his ex-wife. He refers to her as The Bitch. He says he can't believe he was ever involved with her, but blames [it on] being blinded by drugs and alcohol. It's a mistake he never wants to repeat."

The friend says Leigh-Ann is the proverbial bad penny who keeps coming back to haunt Kelsey.

"He said that recently Leigh-Ann had started bugging him about wanting more and more money, now that it was obvious *Frasier* was a hit.

She drives him crazy, and her demands for more money eat him up. But he knew no matter how angry he was at her, he had to stay sober and not let her drive him back to booze.

"He says between the fear he sometimes feels that he may lose the show and his agitation with The Bitch, he started drinking at the awards show—and couldn't stop."

What he didn't share with his fellow alcoholics was his gnawing fear that the scandal surrounding Jane would rear its head at any moment.

It was important for Kelsey to find other outlets for his anxieties, and—whether it is a form of therapy or simply advancing age coupled with less partying—Grammer is actually taking the time to pursue hobbies, like a courtly gentleman professor. It certainly is preferable to embarrassing oneself on national television.

Although few realize it, Grammer is a talented pianist and on occasion will play music to soothe the beasts within his turbulent soul.

"As a rule I sit down at the piano for meditative purposes. I can sit for hours and do it, or sit down for five minutes and do it. I know a couple of standards, like 'When Sunny Gets Blue' and 'Summertime,' but mostly I play what I make up. And the odds aren't great that I'll ever play the same thing twice."

Among his other pleasures are golf, tennis, and gardening. Yes, Frasier Crane tends a vegetable garden.

"Every spring I plant vegetables," Grammer says. "Carrots, corn, radishes—the easy stuff. I just love seeing things growing up out of the ground."

Part of his interest in home-grown food comes from the fact that Kelsey was recently diagnosed with food allergies, and he calls himself a "chemical reactor" when it comes to food additives. But another part is more personal, harking back to when he and his grandfather planted tulip bulbs every fall.

"I loved seeing them come up in the spring. And I still do."

Kelsey laughs at the suggestion that Frasier develop an avid devotion to plants.

"It certainly would make an entertaining show if he became neurotically involved with growing plants. But I don't anticipate any window-box-gardening sketches in the show anytime soon."

His frenetic energy, which was so apparent during the *Cheers* years, seems more focused these days. During rehearsals, Kelsey lies on a couch, cheerleading for other actors as they go through their paces. Unlike Shelley Long before him, Kelsey has never marched his writers into the conference room and demanded they cut down a costar's lines—and laughs. As the California winter sun smiled down on him, for once he seemed a man getting comfortable with being comfortable. He even saw missteps such as the Soap Opera Digest Awards from a better perspective.

But his evolving maturity was due to more than just a hit show, therapy, and regular AA attendance. Kelsey faced the future hopefully because once again his heart had taken the plunge. He was infatuated with a very pretty, very young blonde named Tammi.

But if he thought the gods were finally sending

him a fair wind for his sails, he was sadly mistaken.
He still had more to answer to from days gone by.
He had not heard the last of Jane or her parents—
or the authorities.

NINE

In a case of déjà vu, *Frasier* is shot on the same sound stage that was home to *Cheers* for all those years—at the star's insistence. It gives Kelsey a sense of familiar comfort, and maybe is a reflection of his actor's superstition.

"I do think there's got to be some kind of ghost thing, a support system here," Kelsey muses. "The energy around this stage is wonderful."

So are the warm feelings between the cast members. Grammer has forged an individual relationship with each of his costars and has obvious respect for them all. Even though now he is the show's big cheese (and in fact his costars refer to him as The Big Dog) Kelsey has proven himself to be just as open to suggestion as his *Cheers* producers were with him. Although sometimes he does need convincing.

A case in point is the casting of both David Hyde Pierce and Jane Leeves. When the producers suggested the idea of having an English house-keeper, who is semipsychic, no less, Grammer was initially resistant.

"I thought, 'Oh, my God, it's *Nanny and the Professor*,'" Kelsey recalls. "I didn't want to do *Nanny and the Professor*. But before the rehearsal I had a think and then said, 'OK, you've got to convince me it's not going to be a stereotype and it's not going to be just a silly little device in the show.'"

Leeves read, and she blew him away.

"She certainly did," Grammer admits. "After she was done I immediately said, 'Hire her. That's fabulous.'"

Pierce's character was a late addition to the series and came about thanks to a sharp-eyed casting agent. To be more precise, the character of Niles, Frasier's brother, didn't even exist before casting agent Sheila Guthrie took it upon herself to show the producers a head shot of Pierce and boldly announce, "This is Frasier's younger brother."

David Hyde Pierce's resemblance to Kelsey was striking, but a mere lookalike didn't set off any waves of inspiration for the producers—until Guthrie played them a tape of the canceled series *The Powers That Be*, in which Pierce starred. They signed him right up.

Pierce is a Yale-trained actor with exceptional improvisational skills. In the same way Magic Johnson and Kareem Abdul-Jabbar made each other even more stellar than they already were on the basketball court, Pierce and Grammer feed off each other in the most positive of ways.

From the start, the producers had their eye on John Mahoney, a highly respected actor who had performed both on the stage (and won a Tony for his performance in John Guare's *House of Blue Leaves*) and in films such as *Moonstruck* and *Say Anything*. Although he's only fourteen years older than Grammer, Mahoney had no problem accepting the job.

"It was the best pilot I had ever seen," Mahoney states. "I'd rather do a good sitcom than a bad Broadway play any day. This is the sort of thing anybody with a brain would be proud to be a part of."

In a very real way, the *Frasier* family has become Kelsey's family. Even though they film on the sound stage where he spent a decade working on *Cheers*, this experience is a world apart.

"What's interesting is that in some weird way, *Cheers* feels like it never happened," Grammer has said. "I know it did, and it was a wonderful experience, but it seems so distant, so far away."

Well, there might be one little thing that reminds Kelsey of earlier *Cheers* days, a reminder of past costars who made his days wretched and put a low growl in his voice whenever their names come up—except in this case his nemesis is a four-legged scene-stealer who doesn't have to ask for any lines. His mugging has made him one of television's newest stars.

This, of course, is Eddie the dog, who in real life is known as Moose. On the other hand, what Kelsey calls the canine is not fit for children's ears.

At first it was hard to know whether Kelsey was simply staying in character when asked about his relationship with Moose on and off camera, but friends of Kelsey swear he really, truly, honest to God, cross-his-heart-and-hope-to die, Scout's honor *loathes* the pooch.

A lot of dog fanciers share his feelings toward Jack Russell terriers, who are supremely trainable but have the personality of your snappy old grandma. *Feisty* is an adjective often heard when describing them.

It may have been at Kelsey's gleefully malevolent suggestion that one script was written around the idea of the scene-stealing mutt getting neutered. In the end, however, all it did was center even more attention on him, especially since that show was the second-season premiere. That's showing a lot of confidence in Eddie's drawing power.

"Yes, Eddie's getting the old snip-snip," laughed series creator David Lee. "His love life is coming to a crashing halt."

"Yeah," Peter Casey chimes in, "we'll be using the doggie-cam on that one. We knew we had to do something that's *centered* on Eddie. But even though it's a show about a dog getting neutered, it's really about Frasier and his dad, because Frasier decides to do it without his father's permission. It's another expression of anger and difficulty the dad has in giving up control over his life—and Frasier steps over the line with it."

Grammer would have actually liked to step *on* the little beast.

His lack of devotion toward Eddie has played itself out on the stage and on national television. Shortly after the start of the second season, Kelsey and several cast members flew to New York to appear on the Phil Donahue show. Including Moose.

The talk show host proved to be a dog lover and made a huge fuss over Moose, scratching behind his ears, nuzzling with him, and having the set photographer take a picture of them together. Meanwhile, offstage the *Frasier* publicists were pulling out their hair every time Donahue mispronounced the show's name, saying "Fray-zer" instead of "Fray-zhur."

When the taping was over, a crush of people crowded around Moose, while Grammer tried to hide his irritation . . . sort of. When someone noticed he didn't seem happy and asked if there was some sibling rivalry, Kelsey nearly bit the questioner's head off.

"Of course! Sure there is! Well, it's just so silly— he gets so much attention. I do draw the line when somebody says, 'Oh, he's such a good little actor.' It's just a dog!"

Kelsey slammed a fist on a nearby table to emphasize his point.

"And no, I don't think he has an opinion. Moose pretty much lives for his tricks and his little hot dogs. It's sort of depressing, I know. Once in a while I'll go up and pet him—and he looks around for what he's going to get. If you pet him, he expects a hot dog."

It has actually been suggested that Grammer's frustration over "Moose this" and "Moose that" has escalated to the point where he has sat fuming in his trailer.

"Never—I have never stayed in my trailer and pouted. But Moose has, the little shit."

In less volatile moments, Grammer admits he appreciates the value of an Eddie/Moose, even if he doesn't like it.

"Hey, it takes care of kids a lot. If the dog grabs them, brings them in a little bit, they end up thinking anyway, listening to the show. And then, hey, it's the best of both worlds."

But it's hard for Kelsey to pass up a chance to express his sentiments toward Moose. One day rehearsal was going particularly smoothly and one of the crew members remarked on how rapidly they were moving through the material. The director distractedly commented that they hadn't done any dog scenes, which by their very nature are more time-consuming.

"Good," Kelsey piped up. "Fuck the dog."

It should be noted that on the whole Kelsey is a dog lover supreme, owning six himself (none of them Jack Russell terriers). It's just Moose he doesn't like.

Not everyone shares Kelsey's love-hate war with Moose.

"Actually, he's probably the most disciplined cast member," jokes John Mahoney. "The rest of us are the ones who goof around."

Jane Leeves seems the most in awe over her furry castmate.

"The things he can do are amazing—it's like he's a method actor. I had one scene where I had to scold him and tell him to get off the couch—and for the whole week he was distant and cold to me. I couldn't understand it.

"Later I figured out he was using that anger for the scene. I really respect that."

"Yes, Moose is a true professional and a joy to work with," Grammer says with zombielike enthusiasm.

"We have conflicting styles," David Hyde Pierce says of the dog, tongue firmly tucked in cheek. "But we have mutual respect for one another. I will say I think his range is expanding."

One person whose feelings about Moose are more personal is his owner, Mathilde DeCagney, who is a professional animal trainer. She took Moose, who is now four years old, to an open audition for the role of Eddie, and was delighted when he won the part. But fame did not come without a scare.

"The first time he got in front of an audience, he got skittish," DeCagney recalls. "Still, he just had the right look—and that face. He was really green. This was not old hat to him. So to help compensate for his lack of ability in some areas, the producers made his tricks easier in the beginning.

"He's picked up on acting very fast. He's a quick learner—but I do respect his need for playtime. He knows when it's time to pay attention and rehearse and he knows when it's time to goof off. He understands his limits. He knows he can tire himself out and lose his concentration."

All Grammer knows is that he's being upstaged by the hottest dog star since Lassie. A story often repeated on the set recounts how, shortly after the show's premiere, Kelsey suggested an episode where Eddie commits suicide.

"In the plot, Eddie was to fall in love," says someone close to the production. "Then when the girl dog moves out of town, Eddie pines away for her.

Finally, out of despair, he jumps off the ledge of Frasier's high-rise apartment."

Whether the story is hyperbole or not, it is true that Eddie-mania was an instant by-product of *Frasier*'s success. In more serious moments, both cast and executives admit it was unexpected and not necessarily desired.

"It would be easy for the cast to get sick of this dog's popularity," says Peri Gilpin, who plays call screener Roz Doyle. "One time we all went to a charity event and all everyone wanted to know was, 'Where's Eddie?' It was like, 'How *dare* you show up without him.' I mean, John Mahoney is a Tony winner, but he's now better known as Eddie's dad."

Mahoney says that as Moose's popularity has grown, people tend to chat with him about his performances on the show but almost always want to know where the dog is.

To show just how important Moose has become to the franchise, consider a recent event that had Paramount executives' hearts nearly bursting in their chests. On the lot there is a newly landscaped area that runs the length of the front of the studio lot where it fronts Melrose Avenue. Near the commissary is a rise of manicured lawn that is known as the Grassy Knoll.

It is a sign of an executive's prowess if he or she is one of those who bring dogs to work. Many executives do, and one of the favorite walking spots is the Grassy Knoll because of its proximity to the executive offices.

Late one morning a sudden commotion was heard coming from the direction of the Grassy

Knoll—the frenzied, furious sounds of snarling, biting dogs. Yelping was also heard. Several execs ran out of their offices to see what was going on. There, on the Grassy Knoll, Moose had gotten into a tangle with a much bigger dog over bathroom territory. Several of the executives recognized Moose and ran over to make sure he hadn't been wounded. Forget the fact that whenever a Jack Russell is involved, it's a safe bet not only that he instigated the confrontation but also that he probably more than handled his own.

Moose was indeed a little scraped up, with maybe a tuft or two of fur missing. When the *Frasier* brain trust heard about the dogfight, they nearly went into shock until they had checked Moose from stem to stern.

The close call resulted in an edict from the very upper echelons of the studio. When it is time for Moose to relieve himself, all other dogs must vacate the Grassy Knoll. Let's face it—Moose has achieved Faye Dunaway-like perks.

Despite their hovering protectiveness of Moose, the producers know it's a tricky situation, juggling the hoopla over Moose with their actors' often-fragile egos.

"This isn't *The Eddie Show*," Peter Casey points out. "He's become so popular, of course we were tempted to use him more. But we've decided to use him as a nice little dash of spice every once in a while. We don't want to make him the whole stew. We're realizing a little of Eddie goes a long way."

There has been admitted exasperation at seeing Eddie on magazine covers and doing television talk show appearances. David Angell tries to be sensitive to the nerve Moose may be hitting among his two-legged castmates.

"An actor works all his life to get to a certain position and it's hurtful when someone then comes up and says, 'Hey, love the dog!'"

Grammer would probably be the first to admit it's a losing battle to wage a power struggle against a dog. But as with so many other things in his life, he just can't seem to help himself. When the series first began taping, Kelsey nixed a suggestion to let Moose come out to meet the audience with the rest of the cast before the actual taping started.

But as Eddie became a star in his own right, chants of "Eddie! Eddie!" came from the audience, often so loud as to drown out anything one of the cast might be saying.

"The audiences were screaming so loudly for Eddie, it was positively thunderous," says an eyewitness. Kelsey had no choice but to give in or come across as a kind of grinch. So now Moose is introduced along with the rest of the cast—and often gets the loudest applause. He also gets three times the fan mail Kelsey does.

"Hundreds of requests come in every week for pictures of Eddie. He sends back a standard eight-by-ten signed with the imprint of a dog paw," a source said.

Even Kelsey's own daughter, Spencer, loves Eddie and had her dad get her one of Eddie's paw-printed photos. He drew the line, though, when she asked if she could adopt one of the three puppies Eddie sired with his stand-in, Folie.

"It was bad enough when the *Frasier* Christmas

card ended up showcasing Moose wearing reindeer antlers. There was no way he was going to have any of Moose's offspring living with him, even part-time." the source said.

Since Moose is there to stay, Grammer has tried to make peace with the situation any way he can, and it seems looking at the dog as a financial asset has made him easier to take.

"He's huge," Kelsey concedes. "I just look at it that we're all making money off of him. I don't have a problem with that."

If Moose were the extent of Kelsey's problems, what a sweet life it would be indeed. In the overall scheme of things, Moose's stardom might have offered Kelsey a convenient lightning rod for his pent-up emotions, but in reality it was by far the least of his troubles.

Nor was it problem enough to detract from the one shining light brightening his personal life these days. Tammi Baliszewski, who goes by the last name Alexander, came into Kelsey's life when he was a man about to go under. He says they met shortly—*very* shortly—after his split from Leigh-Ann, in June of 1993 at a bar called Harry O's in Manhattan Beach, a seaside community south of Los Angeles.

As has happened so many times, Kelsey was immediately carried away, but he says that this time he pulled himself up short.

"I thought, well, I really shouldn't do this. I'm not *qualified* to be in another relationship yet. Which was basically true. I had just kicked my ex-wife out, so I wasn't feeling real *good* about myself. The only reason I went out is because my friends had dragged me. They say, 'Kels, you gotta get out. Get rid of the ghosts.'"

Tammi was at Harry O's having a good time with friends after a spirituality seminar. When she looked up, she saw a familiar face looking back at her. She too was immediately attracted, but there was no way she was going to walk over and strike up a conversation. He was a star and might laugh in her face.

"Plus, I'd read about how things weren't going well with him—although he seemed happy and bubbly at the time."

What Alexander did do was smile.

Kelsey noticed. He saw a pretty woman, and in his mind's eye sensed some sadness beneath the surface. Whether real or imagined, it appealed to his sense of longing.

"I sensed something in her, and that attracted me. The last thing in the world I intended was to go over and talk to her. Even in the best of times, there are few things more frightening than approaching a woman. It's like the first time you ask a girl to dance in junior high—and they usually say no. That rejection is just so goddamn painful."

But then he remembered something his old friend George Wendt used to say, and applied it to the current dilemma.

"He'd say, 'You don't have a hair on your ass if you don't go up and talk to that girl.'"

Grammer was nervous and found himself apologizing profusely, asking if he was bothering her. He was a sorry candidate for a new relationship not only because of his newly enacted divorce proceedings but also because of the uncertainty that lay ahead involving Jane. But he just couldn't walk away.

To Tammi's surprise, Kelsey called her the next morning and invited her to a barbecue. In yet another step toward exorcising ghosts, the cookout was being held at the house he had shared with Csuhany.

It was a night all too rare for Kelsey. There were no fights, no accusations of having failed someone, just pleasant company and interesting conversation. His libido had awakened, too.

Tammi got equally carried away beneath the stars that night and found herself thinking in terms of a future life with Kelsey. But for once a sense of caution held Grammer back. There was so much baggage on his train, and it would be unfair to burden Tammi with it.

"He didn't call—not for three months," Alexander recalls. "I was devastated."

"I ran away," Kelsey explains. "I realized immediately that I cared deeply for her, but I just wasn't prepared for a relationship. Not *this* relationship. I had some work to do on my own before I could approach her."

Kelsey thinks it marked a turn in his romantic life. He didn't chase after Tammi, nor did he seek out good-time party girls to fill his nights. For maybe the first time ever, he tried to act like a responsible, thinking adult when it came to a matter of the heart. It was almost a test of faith—the very faith he had lost so many years ago with his sister's death.

"In a way, the minute I said no to the kind of

relationships I'd had before, the universe, God, whoever it is, said, 'Here you go. We've been waiting so long to give you this.'"

This being the solid relationship he felt Tammi had to offer. She was a clean-living health nut who exuded spirituality. He spent hours in therapy answering his own questions about how he should approach this relationship, how to make it different from the others. It's a curious kind of conceit that Grammer assumed Tammi would still be waiting there for him when he was ready to take the plunge.

But she was. In September 1993 Kelsey called Tammi and asked her to be his date to the premiere party for *Frasier*. She readily accepted.

"I had fallen in love with him the first night when he kept apologizing for interrupting me," she admitted later.

They quickly became steady dates, with Kelsey mindful at every step that this one could be the one he'd really, *truly* been waiting for. Over the holidays, Kelsey asked Tammi to go with him on vacation to Mexico. They flew to Puerto Vallarta, still a picturesque town perched near a bay. It's where Elizabeth Taylor and Richard Burton spent many a passionate day and night while filming *Night of the Iguana*.

It was there that Kelsey dared to let Tammi know what he thought their future together held.

"We were looking at this gorgeous, moonlit view. I was wearing an off-white dress, and he looked at me and said I looked like the bride of his heart."

Tammi burst into tears, and Kelsey began to apologize for upsetting her.

"He thought he had scared me somehow," Tammi laughs. "I just stared at him and said, 'Scared me—are you kidding?'"

Not even the news that Kelsey was the focus of an official investigation for statutory rape dissuaded Alexander.

She believed in Kelsey, in his goodness, and couldn't conceive of him as being capable of such a dastardly, sick act. Kelsey was everything she wanted and so much more. He swept her off her feet in a way she thought happened only in romance novels.

Not that everything is sugar-coated.

"Oh, no," Grammer laughs. "We have debates and disagree on various things. We talk about religion, we banter about health—but the bottom line is we have great respect for each other's individuality."

To be able to talk to a well-rounded person, to agree and even to disagree without ducking phones that have been ripped out of the wall . . . it was a whole new world. Kelsey felt that he had overcome something important—that he had finally stopped repeating the same mistakes.

"I think it's your duty to overcome what you inherit in life," he says. "There's a line in *David Copperfield* that says, 'Am I going to be the master of my fate—or its victim?' Well, I'm not going to be its victim, even though I feel like I've been victimized a lot."

His feeling of victimization would reach new depths soon, but for now he saw the world in beautiful, warm colors. He refused to dwell on the investigation—it would only drag him down. He decided to just deal with each day as it came along.

He and Tammi had officially become a couple and were spotted hand in hand, arm in arm, everywhere. Kelsey's life took on an unaccustomed lighthearted air.

In February 1994 Grammer was a participant at the annual Big Brothers bachelor auction, where different eligible bachelors from business, sports, and entertainment are auctioned off, with prearranged date activities, to the highest bidder. The event is a big money-raiser and a lot of fun.

When it was Kelsey's turn to be auctioned off, the bidding was fast and furious. But the ladies in the ballroom didn't stand a chance—it was a fixed contest. Prior to the bidding, he had told Tammi to bid to her heart's content, and when the dust had settled she had "won" him for $15,000.

This prompted one Beverly Hills socialite to sniff pointedly, "She must be doing *very* well in her job as a spokesmodel for an insurance firm to be able to afford that kind of money."

But what nobody at the benefit knew was that Kelsey had already promised his heart and life to Tammi.

"They were out shopping—naturally, driving around in a limo," says a friend, "when all of a sudden, Kelsey slid off the seat onto the floor, so he was kneeling on one knee, and he asked her to marry him. Tammi said yes, although it was something they decided to just keep between themselves for a while."

Later Kelsey would ask again in front of a *Frasier* studio audience.

"I do have a great sense of occasion," Grammer says. "You know how it's not art if it's not in front of people? Well, I think it's not a commitment unless you share it with others. I'm just relieved she still wanted to marry me."

TEN

Tammi says the surprise almost didn't happen.

It was March 22, the last taping day of the season for *Frasier*. Tammi and her mom were supposed to go to the taping.

"It was turning out to be one of the worst days of my life," she says. "My car had been towed and impounded, and I just didn't want to go to the taping that night. I just wanted to go home. But my mom kept pushing me to go. 'Come on, things will get better.'"

What Tammi didn't know is that Kelsey also invited her priest and his own mother. As he always does, Grammer comes out to chat with the audience prior to taping. Standing there, he pointed to Tammi and introduced her.

Tammi recalls wondering what was going on.

"I wasn't wearing any makeup and it was a bad hair day. Then Kelsey drags me in front of all these people in the audience."

To her shock, Kelsey began to talk about their relationship.

"A while ago, Tammi consented to be my wife," he told the surprised audience—and the even more stunned Alexander. The other cast members of *Frasier* were also standing nearby.

"She's made me prouder than I've ever been of myself before. I just wanted to announce formally, in front of the people I'm fond of, and give her this as a token of my affection," he said, slipping a two-carat diamond on her finger. Then he dropped to one knee.

"Just in case you didn't mean it before—will you marry me?"

With her heart in her throat, Alexander told him she would be proud to be his wife.

The audience, and *Frasier*'s cast and crew, roared their approval.

Tammi's mom, Judy Butler, was so happy she was moved to tears. She admits she was in on the plan.

"I knew Kelsey was going to announce their engagement, but I had no idea it would be *so* public. But the way he did it was really cool. Tammi was shocked—pleasantly. Kelsey's discovered what everyone who knows Tammi does—that she's as beautiful on the inside as she is on the outside."

Butler brings up one reason why they haven't gotten married already: Grammer wants his bride to have a church wedding.

"It might take a while for Kelsey to get his marriages annulled through the Catholic Church. Annulments take time because there's a lot of red tape, but he's determined to do it for Tammi. She told him she'd be fine eloping—hopping a plane to the Marriage Mart in Las Vegas for a quickie ceremony. But he won't hear of it. He told her they were going to do it right. I think it's really important for him."

Butler says neither she nor her daughter is concerned about Kelsey's former drug and alcohol problems, and says the way he's handled things has proven a lot to Tammi. "She admires the way he's battled to overcome them."

Alexander can appreciate Kelsey's hard times because she hasn't exactly led the life of Pollyanna, either. Prior to meeting Kelsey, the thirtysomething Tammi lived in Las Vegas and made her living as a nude model, posing for several escort-service ads that are plastered everywhere along the gambling mecca's main strip.

"I did pose nude," Tammi admits. "And it's true my naked body was used to promote prostitution. I regret it, but I needed the money."

In Las Vegas, Tammi went by the name Tammi Jo Baliszewski.

"I'm embarrassed people will think I was an exotic dancer or a stripper in Las Vegas—or even worse," Tammi says. "I was fully aware that some girls I knew were hooking for money, but I was not one of them. I'm just an innocent girl from Kansas caught up in the not-so-innocent Las Vegas lifestyle."

Ironically, while Kelsey worried about all the baggage he was dumping on Tammi in the early days of their relationship, she couldn't figure out how to tell him she wasn't the lily-white flower he thought she was.

"Here I was in love with this wonderful man, yet I hadn't told him anything about my life in Las Vegas," Tammi admits. "I guess I was afraid of being judged."

When she finally built up the courage to tell him, he may have been surprised, but he took it all in stride. After all, this was hardly a man with an unblemished past.

"She's lived," he says simply. "That makes her a whole human being."

"I felt as though a giant weight had been lifted off my back," Alexander says now. Rather than let her whole Las Vegas experience drag her down, it actually helped Tammi get back in touch with her faith. She moved to Los Angeles in 1992 and gave herself a fresh start, using her faith as the springboard.

"I wouldn't say I'm religious," Tammi says, "but I do have a good relationship with God, a good spiritual foundation."

Alexander attends St. Monica's Church in Santa Monica, a city nestled between Los Angeles and the Pacific Ocean, below Malibu.

Her pastor, Father Ken Deasy, echoes Mrs. Butler's comments, repeating that untangling Kelsey's past marital record could take some time. He explains exactly what an annulment means as far as the church is concerned. It is not the same as a legal annulment.

"An annulment determines if the couple was emotionally and psychologically capable of sustaining the marriage in the first place. If not, then the Lord wouldn't choose for them to be together. It puts the past behind them so the new bride and groom can get on with their lives. But it can take more than a year."

Grammer is willing to wait. And until he can marry her in a house of God, he'll satisfy himself with simply knowing they have already exchanged vows in their hearts.

Ever the romantic, Kelsey waxed poetic when speaking of Tammi shortly after their engagement.

"I believe in her—I believe in her word, and that's something I never did with a woman before. Besides, she's beautiful and she has a good heart. I feel that there is fertile ground to cover."

Not everybody is swept away by Kelsey's fairy-tale romance. One skeptical voice comes from someone who's been in Tammi's shoes—Grammer's ex-wife Leigh-Ann Csuhany. Whether she is displaying the resentment of a woman scorned or genuine insight, Csuhany wonders if it is finally true love for Kelsey, or a reversion to type.

"Kelsey hates being alone because he's so insecure," Leigh-Ann says. "He's fine as far as work goes, but actually he's a very insecure person. All I know is that he can't spend any time alone—he's got to have a woman. As soon as we split up he had another woman right there. He wants to be loved so badly."

The hopeful side of Kelsey's soul has always believed that his salvation would indeed be found through the right woman's love. But the journey toward salvation can be fraught with temptations for someone who has spent over half his life chasing alternative states of consciousness. Grammer, though, refuses to flog himself over any stumbles he may have made along the way.

"'Aw, I'm such a bad boy. . . .' No, I don't believe in that. Although there's definitely some bad boys out there!"

Kelsey should know, because whether or not he actively participates in bad-boy activities, in his heart he'll always be a bad boy. But on at least one occasion since his engagement to Tammi, Grammer did play hooky from his rehabilitated ways.

In April 1994 Kelsey painted New York red during a festive evening in which he frequented a number of strip joints and bars. Although by all accounts Grammer has kicked his cocaine habit, he still knows how to party with the best of them when he's left to his own devices in a party pit like New York.

Kelsey was in town to host *Saturday Night Live*, and Alexander was flying out the next day to join him for a few days of fun and shopping. Kelsey had also persuaded the producer of *Saturday Night Live* to give his fiancée a walk-on part. It was going to be a fun few days in the Big Apple.

But Kelsey began the celebration a few nights earlier without Tammi.

After meeting up with two friends, Grammer stepped out to Billy's, a Manhattan strip joint. One of the dancers, Lura Berry, was working that night, and said it was a surprise to see him walk in. But she adds that he was a very attentive customer.

"Kelsey really enjoyed my act," Lura says. "There's one point where I lie on my back and move my legs in a circular motion before doing the splits. I'm topless, but I've got on fishnet stockings and suspenders. Kelsey tipped me quite a bit and told me I had wonderful legs.

"But he really was into another dancer named Betty. I saw him tip her a few times."

Grammer had such a good time at Billy's, he showed up two nights later with a buddy at a Times Square club called Flashdancers.

"It had been a real quiet night," says one of the employees, "but it came to life when Kelsey walked in. He and his friend sat next to the stage and drank a few beers."

Grammer watched a few table dances, in which G-string-clad ladies dance on the customer's table. No touching is allowed. Table dances can be bought for $20. But many of the clubs also offer what's called lap dances, where the girl will "dance" on the customer's lap and perhaps engage in some sexy banter. But again the customer is forbidden to lay a hand on the girl. At risk of losing their licenses, the bars actually enforce the no-sex clause.

"Kelsey asked for our special champagne service," says the employee. "Kelsey and his friend were taken to one of the club's private rooms, where they'd be personally entertained by two of our girls."

Grammer and his buddy enjoyed the entertainment and went through three bottles of champagne, until the club was closing—at four in the morning—and it was time to leave. But apparently Kelsey hadn't bothered to ask the prices.

"He got real upset when he was brought the bill," the employee says. "The champagne was two hundred and fifty dollars a bottle, and it costs a hundred dollars an hour for each girl. With tax, the bill was close to two thousand dollars."

Grammer should have taken it as a sign that he was better off not taking too many walks on the wild side anymore. Not only were they dangerous to his sobriety, but they also put a serious dent in his wallet.

When Alexander arrived the next day, Grammer was happy to see her. They had a wonderful time in New York, and at the party following the show, Kelsey was under total control, sipping from a glass of champagne. He was learning quickly that there was just as much pleasure to be had from knowing his limits as there was in a couple of wild nights out on the town. The difference between this Kelsey and the man who had snorted cocaine and drank until he blacked out was stark.

But was the difference so great? Had the other Kelsey been so out of control and so self-destructive that he would have become sexually involved with a underage girl? That's what authorities in Arizona and New Jersey intended to find out.

One of the last carefree moments Tammi and Kelsey enjoyed was during the summer of 1994, when Grammer invited over a hundred people to an engagement bash at his home. Friends of the couple mingled with NBC executives, who showed up to surprise Kelsey with a brand-new red sports car worth $75,000. It was both a token of their appreciation and a gesture of support for Kelsey, who was still facing the pending sexual misconduct case.

"Not to be cynical, but regardless of whether they believed Kelsey or not, the bottom line to the network and Paramount was that *Frasier* was a huge hit, making the network and studio scads of money. It would be a financial disaster if anything forced the show off the air. It wasn't so much they cared about Kelsey the man, although I'm sure some of them did. It really boiled down to practical business," said a source.

Before the year was over, everyone's loyalty, from network executives down to the crew, would be tested to the limit. The other shoe was finally about to drop.

Not only was New Jersey looking into Kelsey's relationship with Jane, but Arizona officials had been conducting their own probe and in late 1994 released the findings. The floodgates had opened.

Shortly after November 1993, when the charges first surfaced, Kelsey's attorney, Leon Bennett, had arranged for the girl to give a deposition without her parents being present. In the deposition, Jane denied ever having a sexual relationship with Kelsey.

But a year later, after much therapy, she suddenly reversed her position. She now claimed they indeed had had a sexual relationship. She explained her earlier denial by saying she hadn't wanted to hurt Kelsey because she was in love with him. And he had said he was in love with her, too.

Making matter worse, Grammer's half-brother, John, announced publicly that Kelsey was guilty as charged.

"He told me they had sex, and was very pleased with himself," John claimed. "He described her as five foot nine with long brown hair and ravishing looks. And she was smart. He told me how the girl had been baby-sitting for Spencer so they were alone together. He said to her, 'You know what this means. . . .'

"Kelsey planned to marry her but first would have to see her through college and let her have other relationships. Maybe they would get married when he was forty-six and she was twenty-three. I told him he was crazy—she was only fifteen. He could go to jail."

And indeed, statutory rape is still a crime punishable by a jail sentence in most states. John claims that once news of the affair went public, Kelsey tried desperately to cover his tracks.

"I heard him on the phone coaching her on how to deny their affair. And I saw Kelsey take papers out of his briefcase and shred them. Kelsey should just come clean and tell everything.

"If I have to, I'll testify against him."

But John wasn't without his own agenda. He admitted that he and his brother were no longer talking and accused Kelsey of turning his back on him.

"John wanted to be just like Kelsey," says a friend of the family. "Kelsey's world was so exciting."

But John's own Hollywood experience never matched his brother's.

"He had me come out to California to pursue my career—but he never came through with anything," John says.

Grammer was stunned by John's actions and accusations. At an AA meeting, he stood in front of the group and cried.

"He asked us how someone could crucify their own blood," recalls a member who was at the meeting. "He said he had always helped John out by paying his rent and introducing him to people. He was crushed that his brother would turn on him like that."

Equally problematic was a report issued by the Yavapai County sheriff's department in Arizona. Details of the report, while not proving any illegal activity, at the very least showed Grammer guilty of incredibly bad judgment. The sheriff's department released the report on their investigation and offered insight into what the girl's parents believed happened.

"On three separate occasions, the suspect, Kelsey Grammer, allegedly had sexual contact with the victim. The first incident occurred on 7/7/93 at the Summer Set [sic] Hills Hotel in Watchburg [sic], New Jersey. The other two incidents were on 8/28/93 and 8/29/93 at the Enchantment Resort in Sedona, Arizona.

"The relationship between Mr. Grammer and the victim was discovered by the victim's father. This was subsequently reported to the Avondale Police Department on 9/24/93."

The responding officer spoke with the parents and their attorney. Jane was already in a drug rehabilitation facility in Phoenix, so the officer was unable to talk to her at that time. But the parents explained how they had become aware of the affair through the stepmother's conversation with Rudy Hornish.

During the first interview with Jane at her home on March 17, 1994, she admitted she was sexually active but was uncooperative when it came to helping to prosecute Kelsey. But the investigator points out that she had talked to someone.

"Victim did not notify parents but did tell school friends about the incident.

"In conversations with Angie and Judy Vere,

friends of the victim, the stepmother learned that [her daughter] told her friends that at the hotel in New Jersey and again at the Enchantment Resort that she had sex with Kelsey Grammer."

Angie also told police that when Jane got home from New Jersey, she confided she had had sex with Kelsey. She also told Angie she'd had sex with Kelsey in his room during the Arizona trip, including one time when his daughter was in the next room.

"When questioned by her parents about having sex in Sedona, the girl reportedly replied, 'So what if we did?'

"According to the girl, all that had happened in New Jersey and Sedona was that they had 'hugged and kissed.' This was all Mr. Grammer would admit to in a taped telephone conversation [with the stepmother]."

The girl did admit, however, that the Arizona trip had been planned by her and Kelsey while they were still in New Jersey. Kelsey had also given the stepmother his home phone number and a number where he could be reached in the Virgin Islands, "in case the kids wanted to talk" to him.

"It was later learned that Kelsey had also provided both of his phone numbers to the girl. There were two telephone calls placed to the Virgin Islands on July 20, 1993, from the victim's mother's phone.

"A letter from Mr. Grammer was found by Leslie Vere at the Vere residence. This letter was turned over . . . and a copy provided to me. This letter, while not sexually explicit, is sexually suggestive. A name other than Mr. Grammer's is on the return address, although the letter is signed 'Kels.'

"Grammer tells the girl that after he met her he told [the name is blanked out] . . . 'I envy any man that she allows to spend a minute with her.'"

The report just keeps getting worse. At one point it's revealed that after meeting the girl, Kelsey "put his hands on his gonads and made some sexual comments about her." Jane's stepmom told him to cut it out because she was only fifteen.

One of the more bizarre parts of the report is when it details "the plan" Grammer allegedly devised.

"The plan was simply to wait until she finished college, get married, wait a few years, and then have a family."

This is almost identical to what John claimed Kelsey had told him.

"Angie feels that [the girl] is too smart to fall for the line that Mr. Grammer is handing her. However, the girl did tell Angie she was in love with Mr. Grammer."

Angie's older sister, Leslie, added another tidbit from a phone conversation she overheard between the girl and Kelsey.

"Leslie said that as she walked back and forth through the house she could hear the girl talking about sexual intercourse and what they were going to do each other."

The Vere girls also told investigators that Jane had used marijuana and a strong amphetamine called crystal meth, and that she'd hide certain things at their house, including a key from the Enchantment Resort.

Another friend, Lisa Owen, echoes the Veres' story.

"Lisa said that in New Jersey, the girl had told her that she was baby-sitting Spencer. Kelsey came back real late and Kelsey and the girl were talking. They were sitting there having a cigarette and then Kelsey kissed her and then they had sex.

"The girl told Lisa that she had sex with Kelsey when they were in Sedona also. . . . Lisa said that the girl had told her about 'the plan:' after she went to college, she and Kelsey would get married."

Jane had also talked to Lisa about her meeting with Leon Bennett. Lisa remembered asking Jane if she had lied while being interviewed by Bennett, when she denied her affair with Grammer. Jane told her yes, she had lied.

The police found Jane "an articulate, intelligent sixteen-year-old" who, for the most part, was uncooperative.

"When I first spoke with her, she said she had already done an interview with a lawyer, Leon Bennett, and I could get the tape from him. She had his number memorized.

"According to the girl, Kelsey had told her what was going on with her parents and that they had him write her a letter saying he wasn't going to contact her anymore. She said she had already figured out that 'they' had Kelsey write the letter, so she knew they must be trying to 'do something.'"

Jane claimed that the "something" was to sue Kelsey, which is what he told her. The father denied this to the investigator, saying that at that

point in time he had never considered a civil suit—
his primary consideration was prosecuting Kelsey.

"I next asked the girl if she had sexual intercourse with Kelsey Grammer. . . . The girl kind of
laughed and refused to answer the question."

The investigator told her that the Vere girls had
already told him about her confession to them.
Jane denied she had ever directly said to her
friends she had sex with Kelsey—she had just let
them assume it.

"She was just playing a game with them."

The girl finished the interview by telling the
investigator that Kelsey had never lied to her, had
never hurt her physically or emotionally.

"As far as she is concerned, her parents have
done that."

The interview was conducted in March 1993. By
late 1994, Jane was singing a different tune.

In a move that worked to Kelsey's favor, Arizona
authorities deferred to New Jersey and let them take
over the investigation. A grand jury was convened,
and all Kelsey could do was wait it out. He also went
on the offensive. He gave several interviews to deny
the allegations and held firm to his statement that it
was all an attempt to extort money.

"It's an unfortunate but sad truth that the price
one has to pay for fame is having to defend one's
reputation against outright lies," said a statement
released by Grammer's publicity company, Bender,
Goldman, and Helper.

"Mr. Grammer categorically denies the allegations being circulated in the tabloid press. In fact,
the alleged victim has denied in deposition and
under oath any wrongdoing by Mr. Grammer.

"These malicious claims are an obvious attempt to malign Mr. Grammer's character for financial gain."

Esposito, the attorney for the parents, said Kelsey was wrong. "This has nothing to do with extortion. Extortionists do not call the police. No one ever asked Grammer for a red cent."

It came to an abrupt end four days after Grammer's fortieth birthday. On February 25, 1995, Kelsey's teenage accuser stood before a Somerset County grand jury and told all about her alleged affair. The New Jersey grand jury heard one day of evidence in the Kelsey Grammer case. The proceedings, of course, were secret, but it is known that there were witnesses other than the girl. And tapes of twenty-one phone messages from Kelsey to the girl were also introduced. Somerset County prosecutor Nicholas Bissell hinted he was confident an indictment would be handed down.

Esposito had this to say.

"We gave the tapes to the prosecutor to help them. The grand jury will screen them and decide if there is probable cause for an indictment. No reasonable person listening to those messages could conclude that there was nothing going on."

Despite needing only twelve of twenty-three jurors to vote yes in order to indict Grammer, the New Jersey grand jury voted not to indict.

Grammer's criminal attorney, Roy Black—who successfully defended William Kennedy Smith in his rape trial—secured a restraining order in federal court barring the release of the twenty-one phone messages from Kelsey to the girl.

Grammer's ordeal in New Jersey is over.

What Grammer has never addressed is why, even if he is innocent, he would have put himself in a position to even be accused of such a crime.

ELEVEN

As the millennium approaches, Kelsey Grammer stands a changed man.

Although some people believe the old adage that a leopard never changes its spots, there are others who passionately believe Kelsey is the exception to the rule.

"When Kelsey first started going to AA back in 1988, he would just sit there quietly in the background and never say anything," says a fellow meeting-goer. "Sometimes he would show up at a meeting called Artists and Sobriety with the guy who was on *St. Elsewhere*, Ed Begley, who has over a decade of sobriety. But he didn't share and seemed really paranoid.

"But now it's like he's a different person. He works the program, so it'll work in his life. He's still not overly fond of the big meeting full of other celebrities that becomes a big social hour, so he prefers smaller, closed meetings in private homes.

"But he seems to be comfortable in his own skin now. He'll stop by a meeting after work and is very relaxed."

Tammi often shows up with Kelsey.

"I don't think she's in AA, because she doesn't participate, but she's a regular because she's there showing support for Kelsey. And Kelsey's not shy talking about her when he shares. He says Tammi basically saved him from suicide by sticking with him through the worst days of his life. She put up with him when he was weaning himself off of drugs after his divorce, and helped him get back into physical shape, too, by putting him on a diet and getting him back in the gym exercising."

The AA member says Tammi is very health-conscious and that she and Kelsey often work out together in a Studio City gym.

"Tammy has also taught him to meditate and has gotten him back into church. Kelsey says that for a long time he had lost his faith and didn't think God was there for him. But then Tammi reawakened his spirituality and he realized that without God he'd have been dead by now. He might have lost his faith, but God never forgot about him. Having his faith back has made a big difference in helping Kelsey change. He knows he's here for a reason, even if he's not totally sure yet what that reason is.

"Although he's the first to admit it's still not easy. 'It took me so long to get this,' he always says. Kelsey spent so many years trying to get rid of the pain he felt by using drugs—and in the end, the drugs simply caused him that much more pain. But he's learned the most important thing—[the AA program] works if you work it."

Although some in AA are skeptical because Kelsey still drinks on occasion, this friend is not.

"To some people sobriety means control. It takes what it takes."

Looking back, other friends try to explain how Kelsey managed to get himself into such messes, considering his basically good heart and high intellect.

"Kelsey was looking for solace and compatibility, but always ended up empty-handed because he always ended up with girls who didn't really love him for him," says a friend, recalling the *Cheers* years. "They coveted him for his position in life.

"He's actually very traditional in his values of family," the friend believes. "He wants a wife and children and not to be consumed by the Hollywood scene."

For some it may be hard to accept this image of Grammer, for he is someone who lived a very non-traditional lifestyle for so many years while seemingly addicted to stereotypic Hollywood excesses.

"But it's tough in some ways when fame is thrust upon you," the friend says in Kelsey's defense. "It's not easy to deal with being a public figure. It's true, during the heydays of *Cheers*, we were all hounds. Even when Cerlette was in his life, he was a hound. It didn't matter what a girl had upstairs in her head; all that mattered was her body.

"But I can tell you he's not like that anymore. It's not a conquest anymore. He's more into the value of family, compassion and understanding and love.

"Kelsey has had a total turnaround from his wild party days. We all went through that phase. In other words, you go through your twenties. Although for some people, that lasts until forty!"

Despite all the troubles Kelsey endured over the last several years, it says something about the kind of person he is that he has managed to maintain an excellent relationship with Spencer.

Even Leigh-Ann acknowledges that Grammer has earned high marks as a parent.

"He's a *great* father. Spencer is a great kid. I'd rate him a six as a husband—but a ten as a father. He communicates very well and never raises his voice. There's a lot of love and caring there."

Even Buckner, who initially was hesitant to let Kelsey spend too much time with their daughter, Greer, has also seen the change in Kelsey and has recently encouraged him to spend time with the toddler.

"I was afraid to let Greer stay over when Kelsey was married to Leigh-Ann," Buckner admits. Talking about Greer, by the way, does not run afoul of her agreement of silence with Kelsey.

"Leigh-Ann was a miserable, unstable person. She was terribly jealous of Kelsey paying attention to me and his daughter. It was a scary situation."

Buckner says she believes Grammer was genuinely trying to make his marriage to Leigh-Ann work, so the added turmoil caused by Greer's visits was a problem.

"Kelsey told me he didn't want to have to sneak around and see Greer on the sly. So we both agreed that unless he could commit himself to be a father to her, it wasn't a good idea for him to make sporadic appearances in the baby's life. So he didn't see her for over a year."

Like a lot of Kelsey's friends, Buckner credits Tammi with helping him turn his life around and become on a daily basis the kind of person he'd always been in his heart.

"Tammi understands that when you get a person, you get their past as part of the deal—and that's been okay with her," Barrie says with feeling. "She's been very supportive of his relationship with both Greer and Spencer—and even with me.

"Kelsey's become a superdad. He takes Greer and Spencer every other weekend so they can get a chance to play together."

And he's a father who loves to spoil his kids.

"He showers them with gifts," Buckner laughs. "He's always buying clothes and toys. Kelsey recently saw a six-foot-tall stuffed Mickey Mouse and had it delivered to Greer. She absolutely loves it—she uses it as a chair. When he was in Belgium promoting *Frasier*, he saw a cute little squeaky mouse and brought it back as a present. Now she takes it everywhere and tells people it's from her daddy."

But Kelsey is proving to be more than just a checkbook parent. While he has set up trust accounts in Greer's name so that she'll always be financially secure, he also is involved in the everyday interactions that are the foundation of the bond between parent and child. She's a regular visitor on the *Frasier* set—and he frets over her the way any good dad does over his toddler.

"After I moved to the beach with Greer, Kelsey got worried for her safety around the water," Buckner says. "So he's arranged for her to get swimming lessons. At two. But he wants her to know how to swim properly.

"Greer was born at the end of a two-year relationship between Kelsey and me, and even though that is over for good, he has a wonderful relationship with his child. He's a model father."

Whatever else Grammer may be, he's not going to walk around in sackcloth and ashes, forever publicly repenting for misdeeds and mistakes of the past. Instead he tries to put them in perspective and turn them into something positive he can use.

"I certainly don't want a dull life—nor have I had one up to this point," Kelsey says. "You're not very interesting unless you've suffered a little bit. And actors, I'm afraid, if they're to be any good, have to be kind of interesting—or else have a pretty short-lived career."

Grammer also balks at any suggestion he do public-service announcements as part of his new sober lifestyle.

"I would never do that because I don't believe in preaching. Not that way. I don't believe in taking my own personal experience and using that as a recommendation for either doing, or not doing, something. Everybody's got to make a decision about it on their own."

For Grammer, everything has to fit his own personal style. For example, while many in AA would find fault with the fact that he still will enjoy a drink now and then—a glass of champagne, or a Bloody Mary made with sake—Kelsey's definition of sobriety is one of management as opposed to abstinence.

"Yeah, I'll still have a drink once in a while," he says of his remaining vice. Then adds, "And, I mean, sex. I cling to that concept in a pretty serious way. *That* I highly recommend."

Although he is loath to be the next poster boy against drugs, he doesn't mind getting a few jabs in when the target is the competition. When Grammer found out *Home Improvement* star Tim Allen, whose series (which at the time was number one) was pitted head to head against *Frasier* in the 1994–95 season, has also had his share of drug problems and while in his twenties did jail time for selling cocaine, he couldn't resist one comment.

"Ha! I never *sold* drugs."

The battle with *Home Improvement* certainly upped the ante for Grammer's series, and it was a confrontation many predicted would hand him a humiliating defeat. For the first year it was on the air, *Frasier* followed *Seinfeld* in a time slot some people suggested could hold ratings even if half an hour of blank screen were aired. So more than a few eyebrows were raised when *Frasier* more than held its own against *Home Improvement*—and its top-ten status as well. Largely because of the competition, *Home Improvement* lost its number-one ranking for the season, falling to the second spot.

And what does Kelsey think of the other series?

"Can't tell ya," he says briskly. "I don't want to get into a war with those guys. I saw it once, though. And I laughed once.

"The thing is, I am very proud of what we've done on *Frasier*. I love the character and I really like the show. All the business hoopla"—who's number one, how will it affect syndication sales, and so on—"matters to everyone *around* it, but the guys working on the show really want to do a good show.

"I think this show makes a contribution to the quality of life. And I'm proud of that, damn it!"

And although Tim Allen and *Home Improvement* won't be going anywhere soon, what the 1994–95 season proved is that two quality shows can coexist, however uneasily, in the same time slot. More than that, the season also proved that Kelsey Grammer has every intention of staying on the right road.

And Hollywood is beginning to offer him congratulations on a job well done, both on the air and off.

In September 1994 he won an Emmy, but back then there was still the cloud hanging over his life concerning Jane, so he accepted it without his heart being totally free.

In March 1995 Grammer was nominated for an American Comedy Award. His competition was stiff—Tim Allen and *Mad About You* star Paul Reiser. Ironically the presenter was Ted Danson. Kelsey should have seen that as a divine signal—he won.

He walked up to the podium and accepted the award with obvious emotion.

"It's nice to have Ted handing me something— he's the best," Kelsey told the audience as he took the award from Danson.

"This is gratifying because I've had an unfortunate time the last couple of months, although recently I was given some good news. I want to thank Tammi for standing beside me and helping me through this terrible ordeal. Thank you, honey, I love you madly."

Grammer served notice that his past was finally where it belonged—behind him. It was time to move on and seize the rest of his days.

Because the turnaround has been so dramatic, one of Grammer's philosophies bears repeating.

"Experience is the triumph of hope over adversity. In other words, you've been burned so many times you would think you'd just forget it—but you still have hope. Hope springs eternal. And hope only has value if you've known despair.

"You have a chance to fight for something worthwhile. You have an opportunity to make choices that turn your life into something good again. Now that's an accomplishment.

"The stuff that happens to you—the traffic of life, as I call it—does shape us, but it doesn't have to define us. It doesn't have to be what we end up *being*, or the lasting impression that is made by us. I believe that your duty is to prevail, to overcome your inheritance and your environment and so gain something beyond what you were given."

As Kelsey looks ahead, he's finally freed himself of the demons that held him back for so many years. The future is endless in its promise and untold potential. Kelsey has finally gotten to the point where he is truly his own man, unshackled by mistakes of the past. He's ready and anxious to move ahead. He's got a hit series, he is succeeding with the never-ending task of striving for personal peace, and he enjoys the unconditional love of his fiancée.

Grammer is also embarking on a movie career. Though he turned down the starring role in the movie version of the old TV series *Mr. Ed*, he's agreed to star in *Down Periscope*—with a $2 million paycheck.

He's a man who is facing the future with a full plate.

Except for one little thing.

"I could have a little more hair."

EPILOGUE

In July 1995, the teenage girl filed a multimillion-dollar civil suit against Kelsey Grammer. . . .